Nelson-Jones & Nuttall's

TAX AND INTEREST TABLES

1992/93

London
Fourmat Publishing
1992

ISBN 1 85190 167 1

The material reproduced on pages 31–32, 38, 43–45 and 69, which is wholly or partly Crown copyright, is reproduced with the permission of the Controller of Her Majesty's Stationery Office.

© 1988, 1989, 1990, 1991, 1992 Rodney Nelson-Jones & Graeme Nuttall

Published by Fourmat Publishing, 133 Upper Street, London N1 1QP
Printed by Dramrite Printers Ltd, 129 Long Lane, London SE1 4PL

Preface

These tax tables are designed for the use of accountants, lawyers and all other tax or financial advisers. It is hoped that they are clear enough to be useful also to business people and others interested in tax matters. The tables at the back are primarily for litigation lawyers.

In general, the tables consist of data for the past five financial years from 1987/88, and for the forthcoming year, 1992/93. This is not a rigid rule, however, so it has occasionally been varied in the interests of clarity or convenience. Readers will appreciate that the figures for 1992/93, which derive from the Budget Speech of 10 March 1992, are provisional only until the Budget proposals are passed into the Finance Acts 1992.

A feature of this book is its early publication, at the start of May 1992. A consequence is that it cannot incorporate figures or tables that are unavailable in early April.

This is the fifth of a series of annual editions. Following the first edition, the Institute of Taxation has given permission for these tables to be used in its membership examinations.

We wish to record our appreciation to partners and staff at Field Fisher Waterhouse; to Caroline Farebrother, Rebecca Johnson and Anne Sadeau for research; and to Shelley Nadler, Philip Baker and David Wilkinson for reading, checking and commenting.

It only remains to add that, while the book is designed to be accurate and authoritative, it is not intended to amount to or to replace legal or other appropriate professional advice.

10 April 1992

Rodney Nelson-Jones and Graeme Nuttall
Field Fisher Waterhouse
41 Vine Street
London EC3N 2AA

Table of abbreviations

A&M	Accumulation & Maintenance	PEP	Personal Equity Plan
ACT	Advance Corporation Tax	PET	Potentially Exempt Transfer
BES	Business Expansion Scheme	PRP	Profit-Related Pay
CA	Capital Allowances	RPI	Retail Prices Index
CGT	Capital Gains Tax	SAYE	Save As You Earn
CT	Corporation Tax	SA 1891	Stamp Act 1891
CTT	Capital Transfer Tax	SDRT	Stamp Duty Reserve Tax
ESC	Extra-statutory concession	TA	Income & Corporation Taxes Act
FA	Finance Act	TMA	Taxes Management Act
FYA	First Year Allowance	USM	Unlisted Securities Market
IHT	Inheritance Tax	VAT	Value Added Tax
Initial	Initial Allowance	VATA	Value Added Tax Act
IR	Inland Revenue	WDA	Writing Down Allowance
IT	Income Tax	YA	Year of Assessment
MIRAS	Mortgage Interest Relief at Source	1992/93	The tax year 6 April 1992 to 5 April
NI	National Insurance		1993 (and similarly for references
NRE	Net Relevant Earnings for YA		embodying other dates)
PAYE	Pay As You Earn		

Useful addresses and telephone numbers

Capital Taxes Office
Minford House
Rockley Road
London W14 0DF
Tel: (071) 603 4622
FAX: (071) 602 0029

Inland Revenue
Foreign Entertainers Unit
5th Floor, City House
140 Edmund Street
Birmingham B3 2JE
Tel: (021) 200 2616
FAX: (021) 233 3483

Inland Revenue
Public Enquiry Room
West Wing
Somerset House
London WC2R 1LB
Tel: (071) 438 6420
Tel: (071) 438 7772 ("IR" Tax
Guides)

Inland Revenue
Profit-Related Pay Office
St Mungo's Road
Cumbernauld
Glasgow G70 5PR
Tel: (0236) 736121
FAX: (0236) 725959

Inland Revenue
Shares Valuation Division
Minford House
Rockley Road
London W14 0DF
Tel: (071) 603 4622

Inland Revenue
International Division
Room 311
Melbourne House
Aldwych
London WC2B 4LL
FAX: (071) 438 7602

Inland Revenue Library
Reference Room
Room 8 New Wing
Somerset House
Strand
London WC2R 1LB
Tel: (071) 438 6648

Inland Revenue
Business Profits Division
(Employee Share Schemes)
Somerset House
London WC2R 1LB
Tel: (071) 438 7801
FAX: (071) 438 7095

Inland Revenue
Oil Taxation Office
Melbourne House
Aldwych
London WC2B 4LL
Tel: (071) 438 6525
FAX: (071) 438 7602

Inspector of Foreign Dividends
Lynwood Road
Thames Ditton
Surrey KT7 0DP
Tel: (081) 398 4242
FAX: (081) 398 7333

Inland Revenue
The Stamp Office
Adjudication Section (or Information
and Compliance Section)
Ridgeworth House
Liverpool Gardens
Worthing
W Sussex BN11 1XP
Tel: (0903) 288899 (Adjudication
cases); (0903) 700222 (main
switchboard)
FAX: (0903) 288848

Pension Schemes Office
Lynwood Road
Thames Ditton
Surrey KT7 0DP
Tel: (081) 398 4242
FAX: (081) 398 7333

The Secretary
HM Treasury (AP)
Parliament Street
London SW1P 3AG
Tel: (071) 270 5647
FAX: (071) 270 4827

HM Customs & Excise
New King's Beam House
22 Upper Ground
London SE1 9PJ
Tel: (071) 620 1313
FAX: (071) 865 5570

Contents

page

Calendars
1992 Calendar	6
Days from 1 January 1992	6
1993 Calendar	7
Days from 6 April 1992	7

Capital Gains Tax
Rates	8
Reliefs and exemptions	8
Leases	9
Gilt-edged securities	10
Indexation allowances	12

Corporation Tax
Rates	18
Small companies marginal relief	18
Close company abatements	18

Income Tax
Rates	19
Additional rate on trusts	19
Reliefs	20
Wife's earnings election	22
Fixed profit car scheme	22
Car fuel benefit	22
Car benefit	23
Mobile telephone benefit	23
AA standing and running costs	24
Interest on beneficial loans	25
Covenanted payments	25
Small maintenance payments	25
Personal pension schemes	26
Retirement annuities	26
Partnership retirement annuities	27
Schedule D Cases IV & V	28
Schedule E	28
Inland Revenue Tax Guides	29
Flat rate allowances	31
Uniform allowances	33

General
Capital allowances	34
Certificates of tax deposit	35
Interest factor tables	37
Remission of tax	38
Interest on overdue tax	39
Repayment supplements	39
Double tax agreements	40
Exchange rates	43
Retail Prices Index	46
Average earnings index	47

page

Average weekly earnings	47
House price index	48
Share price index	49

Inheritance Tax
Rates	50
Reliefs and exemptions	50
Inheritance Tax tables	51
Capital Transfer Tax tables	52

National Insurance
Benefits	56
Statutory sick and maternity pay	57
Non-taxable benefits	58
DSS leaflets	59
Contributions	61

Stamp Duties
Fixed duties	67
Ad valorem stamp duties	67
Exempt instruments	68
Reliefs	69
Stamp duty reserve tax	69
Capital duty	69

Value Added Tax
Rates	70
Zero-rated supplies	70
Exempt supplies	70
Relevant services	70
Registration limits	71
De-registration limits	71
Fuel for private use	71
European Community	71
HM Customs & Excise Notices & leaflets	72

Tables
Court special account interest rates	74
Special damage interest table	74
Judgment debt interest rates	75
Clearing Bank base rates	75
Multiplier tables	76
Due dates of tax	77
Life expectation	78

Index   79

Calendar for 1992

January
Sunday		5	12	19	26
Monday		6	13	20	27
Tuesday		7	14	21	28
Wednesday	1	8	15	22	29
Thursday	2	9	16	23	30
Friday	3	10	17	24	31
Saturday	4	11	18	25

February
Sunday		2	9	16	23
Monday		3	10	17	24
Tuesday		4	11	18	25
Wednesday		5	12	19	26
Thursday		6	13	20	27
Friday		7	14	21	28
Saturday	1	8	15	22	29

March
Sunday	1	8	15	22	29
Monday	2	9	16	23	30
Tuesday	3	10	17	24	31
Wednesday	4	11	18	25
Thursday	5	12	19	26
Friday	6	13	20	27
Saturday	7	14	21	28

April
Sunday		5	12	19	26
Monday		6	13	20	27
Tuesday		7	14	21	28
Wednesday	1	8	15	22	29
Thursday	2	9	16	23	30
Friday	3	10	17	24
Saturday	4	11	18	25

May
Sunday		3	10	17	24	31
Monday		4	11	18	25
Tuesday		5	12	19	26
Wednesday		6	13	20	27
Thursday		7	14	21	28
Friday	1	8	15	22	29
Saturday	2	9	16	23	30

June
Sunday		7	14	21	28
Monday	1	8	15	22	29
Tuesday	2	9	16	23	30
Wednesday	3	10	17	24
Thursday	4	11	18	25
Friday	5	12	19	26
Saturday	6	13	20	27

July
Sunday		5	12	19	26
Monday		6	13	20	27
Tuesday		7	14	21	28
Wednesday	1	8	15	22	29
Thursday	2	9	16	23	30
Friday	3	10	17	24	31
Saturday	4	11	18	25

August
Sunday		2	9	16	23	30
Monday		3	10	17	24	31
Tuesday		4	11	18	25
Wednesday		5	12	19	26
Thursday		6	13	20	27
Friday		7	14	21	28
Saturday	1	8	15	22	29

September
Sunday		6	13	20	27
Monday		7	14	21	28
Tuesday	1	8	15	22	29
Wednesday	2	9	16	23	30
Thursday	3	10	17	24
Friday	4	11	18	25
Saturday	5	12	19	26

October
Sunday		4	11	18	25
Monday		5	12	19	26
Tuesday		6	13	20	27
Wednesday		7	14	21	28
Thursday	1	8	15	22	29
Friday	2	9	16	23	30
Saturday	3	10	17	24	31

November
Sunday	1	8	15	22	29
Monday	2	9	16	23	30
Tuesday	3	10	17	24
Wednesday	4	11	18	25
Thursday	5	12	19	26
Friday	6	13	20	27
Saturday	7	14	21	28

December
Sunday		6	13	20	27
Monday		7	14	21	28
Tuesday	1	8	15	22	29
Wednesday	2	9	16	23	30
Thursday	3	10	17	24	31
Friday	4	11	18	25
Saturday	5	12	19	26

Easter Day: 19 April. Whit Sunday: 7 June.
Bank holidays: 17 April; 20 April; 4 May; 25 May; 31 August; 25 December; 28 December.

Days from 1 January 1992 (inclusive)

Date	Jan	Feb	Mar	Apr	May	Jun	Jul	Aug	Sep	Oct	Nov	Dec
1	1	32	61	92	122	153	183	214	245	275	306	336
2	2	33	62	93	123	154	184	215	246	276	307	337
3	3	34	63	94	124	155	185	216	247	277	308	338
4	4	35	64	95	125	156	186	217	248	278	309	339
5	5	36	65	96	126	157	187	218	249	279	310	340
6	6	37	66	97	127	158	188	219	250	280	311	341
7	7	38	67	98	128	159	189	220	251	281	312	342
8	8	39	68	99	129	160	190	221	252	282	313	343
9	9	40	69	100	130	161	191	222	253	283	314	344
10	10	41	70	101	131	162	192	223	254	284	315	345
11	11	42	71	102	132	163	193	224	255	285	316	346
12	12	43	72	103	133	164	194	225	256	286	317	347
13	13	44	73	104	134	165	195	226	257	287	318	348
14	14	45	74	105	135	166	196	227	258	288	319	349
15	15	46	75	106	136	167	197	228	259	289	320	350
16	16	47	76	107	137	168	198	229	260	290	321	351
17	17	48	77	108	138	169	199	230	261	291	322	352
18	18	49	78	109	139	170	200	231	262	292	323	353
19	19	50	79	110	140	171	201	232	263	293	324	354
20	20	51	80	111	141	172	202	233	264	294	325	355
21	21	52	81	112	142	173	203	234	265	295	326	356
22	22	53	82	113	143	174	204	235	266	296	327	357
23	23	54	83	114	144	175	205	236	267	297	328	358
24	24	55	84	115	145	176	206	237	268	298	329	359
25	25	56	85	116	146	177	207	238	269	299	330	360
26	26	57	86	117	147	178	208	239	270	300	331	361
27	27	58	87	118	148	179	209	240	271	301	332	362
28	28	59	88	119	149	180	210	241	272	302	333	363
29	29	60	89	120	150	181	211	242	273	303	334	364
30	30	-	90	121	151	182	212	243	274	304	335	365
31	31	-	91	-	152	-	213	244	-	305	-	366

Calendar for 1993

January					
Sunday		3	10	17	24 31
Monday		4	11	18	25
Tuesday		5	12	19	26
Wednesday		6	13	20	27
Thursday		7	14	21	28
Friday	1	8	15	22	29
Saturday	2	9	16	23	30

February				
Sunday		7	14	21 28
Monday	1	8	15	22
Tuesday	2	9	16	23
Wednesday	3	10	17	24
Thursday	4	11	18	25
Friday	5	12	19	26
Saturday	6	13	20	27

March					
Sunday		7	14	21	28
Monday	1	8	15	22	29
Tuesday	2	9	16	23	30
Wednesday	3	10	17	24	31
Thursday	4	11	18	25	
Friday	5	12	19	26	
Saturday	6	13	20	27	

April				
Sunday		4	11	18 25
Monday		5	12	19 26
Tuesday		6	13	20 27
Wednesday		7	14	21 28
Thursday	1	8	15	22 29
Friday	2	9	16	23 30
Saturday	3	10	17	24

May					
Sunday		2	9	16	23 30
Monday		3	10	17	24 31
Tuesday		4	11	18	25
Wednesday		5	12	19	26
Thursday		6	13	20	27
Friday		7	14	21	28
Saturday	1	8	15	22	29

June				
Sunday		6	13	20 27
Monday		7	14	21 28
Tuesday	1	8	15	22 29
Wednesday	2	9	16	23 30
Thursday	3	10	17	24
Friday	4	11	18	25
Saturday	5	12	19	26

July					
Sunday		4	11	18	25
Monday		5	12	19	26
Tuesday		6	13	20	27
Wednesday		7	14	21	28
Thursday	1	8	15	22	29
Friday	2	9	16	23	30
Saturday	3	10	17	24	31

August				
Sunday	1	8	15	22 29
Monday	2	9	16	23 30
Tuesday	3	10	17	24 31
Wednesday	4	11	18	25
Thursday	5	12	19	26
Friday	6	13	20	27
Saturday	7	14	21	28

September				
Sunday		5	12	19 26
Monday		6	13	20 27
Tuesday		7	14	21 28
Wednesday	1	8	15	22 29
Thursday	2	9	16	23 30
Friday	3	10	17	24
Saturday	4	11	18	25

October					
Sunday		3	10	17	24 31
Monday		4	11	18	25
Tuesday		5	12	19	26
Wednesday		6	13	20	27
Thursday		7	14	21	28
Friday	1	8	15	22	29
Saturday	2	9	16	23	30

November				
Sunday		7	14	21 28
Monday	1	8	15	22 29
Tuesday	2	9	16	23 30
Wednesday	3	10	17	24
Thursday	4	11	18	25
Friday	5	12	19	26
Saturday	6	13	20	27

December					
Sunday		5	12	19	26
Monday		6	13	20	27
Tuesday		7	14	21	28
Wednesday	1	8	15	22	29
Thursday	2	9	16	23	30
Friday	3	10	17	24	31
Saturday	4	11	18	25	

Easter Day: 11 April. Whit Sunday: 30 May.
Bank holidays: 9 April; 12 April; 3 May; 31 May; 30 August; 27 December; 28 December.

Days from 6 April 1992 (inclusive)

Add 5 to get days from 1 April 1992

Date	Apr 92	May 92	Jun 92	Jul 92	Aug 92	Sept 92	Oct 92	Nov 92	Dec 92	Jan 93	Feb 93	Mar 93	Apr 93
1	-	26	57	87	118	149	179	210	240	271	302	330	361
2	-	27	58	88	119	150	180	211	241	272	303	331	362
3	-	28	59	89	120	151	181	212	242	273	304	332	363
4	-	29	60	90	121	152	182	213	243	274	305	333	364
5	-	30	61	91	122	153	183	214	244	275	306	334	365
6	1	31	62	92	123	154	184	215	245	276	307	335	
7	2	32	63	93	124	155	185	216	246	277	308	336	
8	3	33	64	94	125	156	186	217	247	278	309	337	
9	4	34	65	95	126	157	187	218	248	279	310	338	
10	5	35	66	96	127	158	188	219	249	280	311	339	
11	6	36	67	97	128	159	189	220	250	281	312	340	
12	7	37	68	98	129	160	190	221	251	282	313	341	
13	8	38	69	99	130	161	191	222	252	283	314	342	
14	9	39	70	100	131	162	192	223	253	284	315	343	
15	10	40	71	101	132	163	193	224	254	285	316	344	
16	11	41	72	102	133	164	194	225	255	286	317	345	
17	12	42	73	103	134	165	195	226	256	287	318	346	
18	13	43	74	104	135	166	196	227	257	288	319	347	
19	14	44	75	105	136	167	197	228	258	289	320	348	
20	15	45	76	106	137	168	198	229	259	290	321	349	
21	16	46	77	107	138	169	199	230	260	291	322	350	
22	17	47	78	108	139	170	200	231	261	292	323	351	
23	18	48	79	109	140	171	201	232	262	293	324	352	
24	19	49	80	110	141	172	202	233	263	294	325	353	
25	20	50	81	111	142	173	203	234	264	295	326	354	
26	21	51	82	112	143	174	204	235	265	296	327	355	
27	22	52	83	113	144	175	205	236	266	297	328	356	
28	23	53	84	114	145	176	206	237	267	298	329	357	
29	24	54	85	115	146	177	207	238	268	299	-	358	
30	25	55	86	116	147	178	208	239	269	300	-	359	
31	-	56	-	117	148	-	209	-	270	301	-	360	

Capital Gains Tax

Rates

	1987/88	1988/89	1989/90	1990/91	1991/92	1992/93
Individuals	30%	25% & 40%*	25% & 40%*	25% & 40%*	25% & 40%*	20%, 25% & 40%*
Discr & A & M trustees	30%	35%	35%	35%	35%	35%
PRs and other trustees	30%	25%	25%	25%	25%	25%
Annual exemption†	£6,600	£5,000	£5,000	£5,000	£5,500	£5,800

* ie at the marginal rate/s of income tax.

† Available in full to individuals, personal representatives (in year of death and up to two succeeding years) and trustees for mentally disabled persons and those receiving attendance allowances (subject to division among qualifying settlements). Available as to 50% to trustees generally (eg £2,900 in 1992/93) (subject to division among qualifying settlements). The annual exemption cannot be carried forward if unused. Spouses are each entitled to one exemption (from 1990/91).

Reliefs and exemptions

The following is a checklist of the main reliefs and exemptions:
- *Annual exemption* - see Table above.
- *Business Expansion Scheme* (shares issued after 18.3.86 until 31.12.93) - no gain no loss provided income tax relief not withdrawn from shareholder (continues after abolition of income tax relief for BES issues).
- *Charities* - gains exempt.
- *Chattels* disposed of for £6,000 (for 1988/89 and earlier, £3,000) or less - gains exempt.
- *Chattels* disposed of for over £6,000 (for 1988/89 and earlier, £3,000) - gain restricted to 5/3 x (proceeds minus limit (eg £6,000 from 1989/90)).
- *Compensation or damages for personal injury* - exempt.
- *Death* - a tax free uplift.
- *Foreign currency for personal expenditure* - no gain no loss.
- *Gifts* - hold-over relief available (but restricted from 14.3.89 to gifts of business assets, gifts on which there is an immediate charge to IHT and certain other gifts).
- *Gilts* - gains exempt from 2.7.86 (previously subject to CGT when disposed of within 12 months of acquisition). See pages 10 and 11.
- *Indexation allowance* - see Tables on pages 12 to 17.
- *Married couples living together* - no gain no loss on disposals from one to the other.
- *Motor vehicles* - no gain no loss.
- *PEPs* - no CGT charge.
- *Principal private residence and grounds* - gains exempt provided period of residence and other conditions met (dependent relative exemption not available for disposals after 5.4.88 subject to transitional provisions). From 19.3.91 the grounds normally treated as exempt increase from 1 acre to half a hectare.
- *Partly let private residence* - gains exempt on let part, up to lesser of £40,000 for disposals from 19.3.91 (from 6.4.83 to 18.3.91 £20,000) and exemption on owner-occupied part.
- *Qualifying corporate bonds* - gains exempt from 2.7.86 (previously gilts exemption applied to bonds acquired after 13.3.84) (extended to non-convertible sterling bonds generally from 14.3.89).
- *Retirement relief* - maximum exemption on £150,000 gains (in 1985/86 and 1986/87 - £100,000; from 6.4.87 to 18.3.91 - £125,000) and a further 50% relief on gains on disposals from 19.3.91 between £150,000 and £600,000 if aged 55 or over (from 6.4.88 to 18.3.91, 50% relief on gains between £125,000 and £500,000 if aged 60 or over) (or retiring early due to ill health) and 10 year qualifying period.

Capital Gains Tax

Leases

There is a curved line restriction of allowable expenditure on leases which are wasting assets. The excluded expenditure is a fraction of that expenditure which is equal to $\frac{P(1) - P(3)}{P(1)}$ or, as the case may be, $\frac{P(2) - P(3)}{P(2)}$

Where:
P(1) = the percentage (see table below) for the duration of the lease at its acquisition;
P(2) = the percentage for the duration of the lease when expenditure is first reflected in the nature of the lease;
P(3) = the percentage for the duration of the lease at disposal.

For inexact periods take the percentage for the whole number of years plus one twelfth of the difference between that and the percentage for the next higher number of years for each odd month (counting an odd 14 days or more as one month):

Rounding up on 0.00050:-

Years	Months	1	2	3	4	5	6	7	8	9	10	11
50	100.000	100.000	100.000	100.000	100.000	100.000	100.000	100.000	100.000	100.000	100.000	100.000
49	99.657	99.686	99.714	99.743	99.771	99.800	99.829	99.857	99.886	99.914	99.943	99.971
48	99.289	99.320	99.350	99.381	99.412	99.442	99.473	99.504	99.534	99.565	99.596	99.626
47	98.902	98.934	98.967	98.999	99.031	99.063	99.095	99.128	99.160	99.192	99.225	99.257
46	98.490	98.524	98.559	98.593	98.627	98.662	98.696	98.730	98.765	98.799	98.833	98.868
45	98.059	98.095	98.131	98.167	98.203	98.239	98.274	98.310	98.346	98.382	98.418	98.454
44	97.595	97.634	97.672	97.711	97.750	97.788	97.827	97.866	97.904	97.943	97.982	98.020
43	97.107	97.148	97.188	97.229	97.270	97.310	97.351	97.392	97.432	97.473	97.514	97.554
42	96.593	96.636	96.679	96.722	96.764	96.807	96.850	96.893	96.936	96.978	97.021	97.064
41	96.041	96.087	96.133	96.179	96.225	96.271	96.317	96.363	96.409	96.455	96.501	96.547
40	95.457	95.506	95.554	95.603	95.652	95.700	95.749	95.798	95.846	95.895	95.944	95.992
39	94.842	94.893	94.944	94.996	95.047	95.098	95.149	95.201	95.252	95.303	95.354	95.406
38	94.189	94.243	94.298	94.352	94.407	94.461	94.516	94.570	94.624	94.679	94.733	94.788
37	93.497	93.555	93.612	93.670	93.728	93.785	93.843	93.901	93.958	94.016	94.074	94.131
36	92.761	92.822	92.884	92.945	93.006	93.068	93.129	93.190	93.252	93.313	93.374	93.436
35	91.981	92.046	92.111	92.176	92.241	92.306	92.371	92.436	92.501	92.566	92.631	92.696
34	91.156	91.225	91.293	91.362	91.431	91.500	91.569	91.637	91.706	91.775	91.843	91.912
33	90.280	90.353	90.426	90.499	90.572	90.645	90.718	90.791	90.864	90.937	91.010	91.083
32	89.354	89.431	89.508	89.586	89.663	89.740	89.817	89.894	89.971	90.049	90.126	90.203
31	88.371	88.453	88.535	88.617	88.699	88.781	88.862	88.944	89.026	89.108	89.190	89.272
30	87.330	87.417	87.504	87.590	87.677	87.764	87.851	87.937	88.024	88.111	88.197	88.284
29	86.226	86.318	86.410	86.502	86.594	86.686	86.778	86.870	86.962	87.054	87.146	87.238
28	85.053	85.151	85.249	85.346	85.444	85.542	85.639	85.737	85.835	85.933	86.031	86.128
27	83.816	83.919	84.022	84.125	84.228	84.331	84.435	84.538	84.641	84.744	84.847	84.950
26	82.496	82.606	82.716	82.826	82.936	83.046	83.156	83.266	83.376	83.486	83.596	83.706
25	81.100	81.216	81.333	81.449	81.565	81.682	81.798	81.914	82.031	82.147	82.263	82.380
24	79.622	79.745	79.868	79.991	80.115	80.238	80.361	80.484	80.607	80.731	80.854	80.977
23	78.055	78.186	78.316	78.447	78.577	78.708	78.839	78.969	79.100	79.230	79.361	79.491
22	76.339	76.482	76.625	76.768	76.911	77.054	77.197	77.340	77.483	77.626	77.769	77.912
21	74.635	74.777	74.919	75.061	75.203	75.345	75.487	75.629	75.771	75.913	76.055	76.197
20	72.770	72.925	73.081	73.236	73.392	73.547	73.702	73.858	74.013	74.169	74.324	74.480
19	70.791	70.956	71.121	71.286	71.451	71.616	71.781	71.945	72.110	72.275	72.440	72.605
18	68.697	68.871	69.046	69.220	69.395	69.569	69.744	69.919	70.093	70.268	70.442	70.617
17	66.470	66.656	66.841	67.027	67.212	67.398	67.583	67.769	67.955	68.140	68.326	68.511
16	64.116	64.312	64.508	64.704	64.901	65.097	65.293	65.489	65.685	65.882	66.078	66.274
15	61.617	61.825	62.034	62.242	62.450	62.658	62.867	63.075	63.283	63.491	63.699	63.908
14	58.971	59.191	59.412	59.633	59.853	60.073	60.294	60.515	60.735	60.955	61.176	61.397
13	56.167	56.401	56.634	56.868	57.102	57.335	57.569	57.803	58.036	58.270	58.504	58.737
12	53.191	53.439	53.687	53.935	54.183	54.431	54.679	54.927	55.175	55.423	55.671	55.919
11	50.038	50.301	50.564	50.826	51.089	51.352	51.615	51.877	52.140	52.403	52.666	52.928
10	46.695	46.974	47.252	47.531	47.809	48.088	48.367	48.645	48.924	49.202	49.481	49.759
9	43.154	43.449	43.744	44.039	44.334	44.629	44.925	45.220	45.515	45.810	46.105	46.400
8	39.399	39.712	40.025	40.338	40.651	40.964	41.277	41.589	41.902	42.215	42.528	42.841
7	35.414	35.746	36.078	36.410	36.742	37.074	37.406	37.739	38.071	38.403	38.735	39.067
6	31.195	31.547	31.898	32.250	32.601	32.953	33.304	33.656	34.008	34.359	34.711	35.062
5	26.722	27.095	27.468	27.840	28.213	28.586	28.959	29.331	29.704	30.077	30.450	30.822
4	21.983	22.378	22.773	23.168	23.563	23.958	24.352	24.747	25.142	25.537	25.932	26.327
3	16.959	17.378	17.796	18.215	18.634	19.052	19.471	19.890	20.308	20.727	21.146	21.564
2	11.629	12.073	12.517	12.962	13.406	13.850	14.294	14.738	15.182	15.626	16.071	16.515
1	5.983	6.454	6.924	7.395	7.865	8.336	8.806	9.277	9.747	10.218	10.688	11.159
0	0.000	0.499	0.997	1.496	1.994	2.493	2.992	3.490	3.989	4.487	4.986	5.484

Gilt-edged Securities

	Description	Interest	
2.00%	Index-Linked Treasury Stock 1992 †	*23M*	23S
8.00%	Treasury Loan 1992 †	*13A*	13O
10.50%	Treasury Convertible Stock 1992 †	*7M*	7N
3.00%	Treasury Stock 1992	*11J*	11D
12.25%	Exchequer Stock 1992	25F	*25A*
13.50%	Exchequer Stock 1992	22M	*22S*
8.25%	Treasury Stock 1993	*18F*	18A
10.00%	Treasury Loan 1993 †	*15A*	15O
12.50%	Treasury Loan 1993 †	14J	*14J*
6.00%	Funding Loan 1993 †	15M	*15S*
13.75%	Treasury Loan 1993 †	23M	*23N*
8.50%	Treasury Stock 1994	*3F*	3A
14.50%	Treasury Loan 1994 †	*1M*	1S
13.50%	Exchequer Stock 1994	*27A*	27O
2.00%	Index-Linked Treasury Stock 1994	*16M*	16N
10.00%	Treasury Loan 1994 †	*9J*	9D
12.50%	Exchequer Stock 1994	22F	*22A*
9.00%	Treasury Loan 1994†	17M	*17N*
12.00%	Treasury Stock 1995	*25J*	25J
10.25%	Exchequer Stock 1995	21J	*21J*
12.75%	Treasury Loan 1995 †	15M	*15N*
14.00%	Treasury Stock 1996	*22J*	22J
9.00%	Treasury Loan 1992-96 †	*15M*	15S
15.25%	Treasury Loan 1996 †	*3M*	3N
13.25%	Exchequer Loan 1996 †	*15M*	15N
2.00%	Index-Linked Treasury Stock 1996	16M	*16S*
10.00%	Conversion Stock 1996	15M	*15N*
13.25%	Treasury Loan 1997 †	*22J*	22J
10.50%	Exchequer Stock 1997	*21F*	21A
8.75%	Treasury Loan 1997 †	1M	*1S*
15.00%	Exchequer Stock 1997	27A	*27O*
9.75%	Exchequer Stock 1998	*19J*	19J
6.75%	Treasury Loan 1995-98 †	*1M*	1N
15.50%	Treasury Loan 1998 †	30M	*30S*
12.00%	Exchequer Stock 1998	20M	*20N*
9.50%	Treasury Loan 1999 †	*15J*	15J
12.25%	Exchequer Stock 1999	*26M*	26S
10.50%	Treasury Stock 1999	*19M*	19N
10.25%	Conversion Stock 1999	22M	*22N*
2.50%	Index-Linked Treasury Convertible Stock 1999	22M	*22N*
8.50%	Treasury Loan 2000 †	*28J*	28J
9.00%	Conversion Stock 2000 †	*3M*	3S
13.00%	Treasury Stock 2000	14J	*14J*
10.00%	Treasury Stock 2001	*26F*	26A
14.00%	Treasury Stock 1998-2001	*22M*	22N
9.50%	Conversion Loan 2001 †	12J	*12J*
9.75%	Conversion Stock 2001	10F	*10A*
2.50%	Index-Linked Treasury Stock 2001	24M	*24S*

	Description	Interest		
	Description	*Interest*		

Rate	Description			
12.00%	Exchequer Stock 1999-2002	*22J*	22J	
10.00%	Conversion Stock 2002	*11A*	11O	
9.50%	Conversion Stock 2002	*14J*	14D	
9.75%	Treasury Stock 2002	27F	*27A*	
9.00%	Exchequer Stock 2002	19M	*19N*	
9.75%	Conversion Stock 2003 †	*7M*	7N	
2.50%	Index-Linked Treasury Stock 2003	*20M*	20N	
13.75%	Treasury Stock 2000-03	25J	*25J*	
10.00%	Treasury Stock 2003	8M	*8S*	
11.50 %	Treasury Stock 2001-04	*19M*	19S	
10.00%	Treasury Stock 2004	*18M*	18N	
3.50%	Funding Stock 1999-2004	14J	*14J*	
9.50%	Conversion Stock 2004	25A	*25O*	
9.50%	Conversion Stock 2005	*18A*	18O	
10.50%	Exchequer Stock 2005	20M	*20S*	
12.50%	Treasury Stock 2003-05	21M	*21N*	
2.00%	Index-Linked Treasury Stock 2006	19J	*19J*	
8.00%	Treasury Loan 2002-06 †	5A	*5O*	
9.75%	Conversion Stock 2006	15M	*15N*	
11.75%	Treasury Stock 2003-7	*22J*	22J	
8.50%	Treasury Loan 2007 †	16J	*16J*	
13.50%	Treasury Stock 2004-08	*26M*	26S	
9.00%	Treasury Loan 2008 †	13A	*13O*	
8.00%	Treasury Stock 2009	25M	*25S*	
2.50%	Index-Linked Treasury Stock 2009	*20M*	20N	
9.00%	Conversion Loan 2011 †	12J	*12J*	
2.50%	Index-Linked Treasury Stock 2011	23F	*23A*	
9.00%	Treasury Stock 2012	6F	*6A*	
5.50%	Treasury Stock 2008-12 †	10M	*10S*	
2.50%	Index-Linked Treasury Stock 2013	16F	*16A*	
7.75%	Treasury Loan 2012-15 †	*26J*	26J	
2.50%	Treasury Stock 1986-2016	*15M*	15S	
2.50%	Index-Linked Treasury Stock 2016	26J	*26J*	
12.00%	Exchequer Stock 2013-17	12J	*12D*	
2.50%	Index-Linked Treasury Stock 2020	*16A*	16O	
2.50%	Index-Linked Treasury Stock 2024 †	17J	*17J*	
4.00%	Consolidated Loan	*1F*	1A	
3.50%	War Loan †	1J	*1D*	
3.50%	Conversion Loan	*1A*	1O	
3.00%	Treasury Stock	*5A*	5O	
2.50%	Consolidated Stock	5J	*5A*	5J 5O
2.50%	Treasury Stock	*1A*	1O	
2.50%	Annuities	*5J*	5A	5J 5O
2.75%	Annuities	*5J*	5A	5J 5O

Securities issued by certain public corporations

3.00%	North of Scotland Electricity Stock 1989-92	*1F*	1A
3.00%	Exchequer (formerly British Gas) Stock 1990-95	*1M*	1N

The list does not cover "A", "B" and "C" Stocks. Redemption day is shown in *italics* in the interest column.

† Interest is exempt from income tax if beneficially owned by a person not ordinarily resident in the UK.

1J	1J	1 Jan	1 July	1A	1O	1 Apr	1 Oct
1F	1A	1 Feb	1 Aug	1M	1N	1 May	1 Nov
1M	1S	1 Mar	1 Sep	1J	1D	1 June	1 Dec
5J	5A	5 Jan	5 Apr	5J	5O	5 July	5 Oct *and so on*

Indexation factors. Left block = disposal during 1982 (Jan–Dec); right block = disposal during 1983 (Jan–Dec). Row label RI = RPI reference month.

RI	1982 Jan	Feb	Mar	Apr	May	Jun	Jul	Aug	Sep	Oct	Nov	Dec	1983 Jan	Feb	Mar	Apr	May	Jun	Jul	Aug	Sep	Oct	Nov	Dec
1982																								
Mar				.020	.027	.030	.031	.031	.030	.035	.041	.039	.040	.044	.046	.061	.065	.068	.074	.078	.083	.087	.091	.094
Apr					.007	.010	.010	.011	.010	.015	.020	.018	.019	.024	.026	.040	.044	.047	.053	.057	.062	.066	.069	.072
May						.003	.003	.003	.003	.008	.013	.011	.012	.016	.018	.033	.037	.039	.045	.050	.054	.058	.062	.065
Jun							.000	.001	.000	.005	.010	.008	.009	.014	.015	.030	.034	.037	.042	.047	.051	.055	.059	.062
Jul								.000	.000	.005	.010	.008	.009	.013	.015	.029	.034	.036	.042	.046	.051	.055	.059	.061
Aug									.000	.004	.009	.007	.009	.013	.015	.029	.033	.036	.041	.046	.051	.054	.058	.061
Sep										.005	.010	.008	.009	.014	.015	.030	.034	.037	.042	.047	.051	.055	.059	.062
Oct											.005	.003	.004	.009	.010	.025	.029	.031	.037	.042	.046	.050	.054	.056
Nov												.000	.000	.004	.006	.020	.024	.026	.032	.036	.041	.045	.048	.051
Dec													.001	.006	.007	.022	.026	.028	.034	.038	.043	.047	.050	.053
1983																								
Jan														.004	.006	.020	.025	.027	.033	.037	.042	.045	.049	.052
Feb															.002	.016	.020	.023	.028	.033	.037	.041	.045	.047
Mar																.014	.018	.021	.026	.031	.035	.039	.043	.045
Apr																	.004	.007	.012	.017	.021	.025	.028	.031
May																		.002	.008	.012	.017	.020	.024	.027
Jun																			.005	.010	.014	.018	.022	.024
Jul																				.004	.009	.012	.016	.019
Aug																					.004	.008	.012	.014
Sep																						.004	.007	.010
Oct																							.004	.006
Nov																								.003
Dec																								

Indexation allowance:
Table of indexation factors

The indexation allowance on a disposal is the total of the indexed rise in each item of relevant allowable expenditure. The indexation factors in this table are calculated as follows:

$$\frac{(RD - RI)}{RI}$$

where: RD is the RPI figure for the month of disposal and RI is the RPI figure for March 1982, or the month in which the expenditure was incurred, whichever is the later (for disposals by individuals prior to 6 April 1985 (1 April 1985 for companies) the RI month is the 12th month after the expenditure was incurred or March 1982, whichever is the later).

There are special rules for the accrued income scheme.

The indexed rise is then calculated as follows:

$$\begin{array}{l}\text{amount of allowable expenditure} \\ \text{(or, if applicable, market value on 31 March 1982)} \end{array} \times \begin{array}{l}\text{indexation} \\ \text{factor}\end{array}$$

For disposals on or after 6 April 1988 of assets held on 31 March 1982 the indexation allowance is calculated, without the need for a claim, on the greater of the allowable expenditure on the asset or the market value on 31 March 1982. If an election has effect, re-basing in all cases to 31 March 1982 values, then the allowance is calculated on 31 March 1982 values.

1984

	Jan	Feb	Mar	Apr	May	Jun	Jul	Aug	Sep	Oct	Nov	Dec
	.093	.098	.101	.116	.120	.123	.122	.132	.134	.141	.145	.144
	.072	.076	.079	.094	.098	.101	.099	.110	.112	.119	.122	.121
	.064	.068	.072	.086	.090	.093	.092	.102	.104	.111	.114	.113
	.061	.065	.069	.083	.087	.090	.089	.099	.101	.108	.111	.110
	.061	.065	.068	.083	.087	.089	.088	.098	.101	.107	.111	.110
	.060	.065	.068	.082	.086	.089	.088	.098	.100	.107	.110	.110
	.061	.065	.069	.083	.087	.090	.089	.099	.101	.108	.111	.110
	.056	.060	.063	.078	.082	.084	.083	.093	.096	.102	.106	.105
	.051	.055	.058	.072	.076	.079	.078	.088	.090	.097	.100	.099
	.053	.057	.060	.074	.078	.081	.080	.090	.092	.099	.102	.101
	.051	.056	.059	.073	.077	.080	.079	.089	.091	.098	.101	.100
	.047	.051	.054	.068	.072	.075	.074	.084	.086	.093	.096	.095
	.045	.049	.052	.066	.070	.073	.072	.082	.084	.091	.094	.093
	.030	.035	.038	.052	.056	.058	.057	.067	.069	.076	.079	.078
	.026	.030	.034	.047	.051	.054	.053	.063	.065	.071	.075	074
	.024	.028	.031	.045	.049	.051	.050	.060	.062	.069	.072	.071
	.018	.022	.026	.039	.043	.046	.045	.054	.056	.063	.066	.065
	.014	.018	.021	.035	.038	.041	.040	.050	.052	.058	.062	.061
	.009	.013	.016	.030	.034	.037	.035	.045	.047	.054	.057	.056
	.006	.010	.013	.026	.030	.033	.032	.041	.043	.050	.053	.052
	.002	.006	.009	.023	.027	.029	.028	.038	.040	.046	.049	.049
	.000	.004	.007	.020	.024	.027	.025	.035	.037	.043	.047	.046
		.004	.007	.021	.025	.027	.026	.036	.038	.044	.047	.046
		.003	.017	.020	.023	.022	.031	.033	.040	.043	.042	
			.013	.017	.020	.019	.028	.030	.037	.040	.039	
				.004	.006	.005	.015	.017	.023	.026	.025	
					.003	.001	.011	.013	.019	.022	.021	
						.000	.008	.010	.016	.020	.019	
							.009	.011	.018	.021	.020	
								.002	.008	.011	.010	
									.006	.009	.008	
										.003	.002	
											.000	

1985

	Jan	Feb	Mar	Apr	May	Jun	Jul	Aug	Sep	Oct	Nov	Dec	
	.148	.157	.168	.193	.198	.201	.199	.202	.201	.203	.207	.209	**1982** Mar
	.125	.135	.145	.170	.175	.177	.175	.178	.178	.180	.184	.185	Apr
	.117	.126	.137	.161	.166	.169	.167	.170	.169	.171	.175	.177	May
	.114	.123	.134	.158	.163	.166	.164	.167	.166	.168	.172	.173	June
	.114	.123	.133	.158	.163	.165	.163	.166	.166	.167	.172	.173	Jul
	.114	.123	.133	.157	.162	.165	.163	.166	.165	.167	.171	.173	Aug
	.114	.123	.134	.158	.163	.166	.164	.167	.166	.168	.172	.173	Sep
	.109	.118	.128	.152	.157	.160	.158	.161	.160	.162	.166	.168	Oct
	.103	.112	.123	.147	.152	.154	.152	.155	.155	.156	.160	.162	Nov
	.105	.114	.125	.149	.154	.156	.154	.157	.157	.159	.163	.164	Dec
	.104	.113	.123	.147	.153	.155	.153	.156	.155	.157	.161	.163	**1983** Jan
	.099	.108	.119	.142	.148	.150	.148	.151	.150	.152	.156	.158	Feb
	.097	.106	.116	.140	.145	.148	.146	.149	.148	.150	.154	.156	Mar
	.082	.091	.101	.125	.130	.132	.130	.133	.132	.134	.138	.140	Apr
	.078	.086	.096	.120	.125	.127	.125	.128	.128	.129	.133	.135	May
	.075	.084	.094	.117	.122	.125	.122	.125	.125	.127	.131	.132	Jun
	.069	.078	.088	.111	.116	.119	.116	.119	.119	.121	.125	.126	Jul
	.064	.073	.083	.106	.111	.114	.112	.114	.114	.116	.120	.121	Aug
	.060	.068	.078	.101	.106	.109	.107	.110	.109	.111	.115	.116	Sep
	.056	.065	.075	.097	.102	.105	.103	.106	.105	.107	.111	.112	Oct
	.052	.061	.071	.094	.099	.101	.099	.102	.101	.103	.107	.108	Nov
	.050	.058	.068	.091	.096	.098	.096	.099	.098	.100	.104	.105	Dec
	.050	.059	.069	.091	.096	.099	.097	.100	.099	.101	.104	.106	**1984** Jan
	.046	.054	.064	.087	.092	.094	.092	.095	.094	.096	.100	.101	Feb
	.043	.051	.061	.083	.088	.091	.089	.092	.091	.093	.096	.098	Mar
	.029	.037	.047	.069	.074	.076	.074	.077	.077	.078	.082	.084	Apr
	.025	.033	.043	.065	.070	.072	.070	.073	.073	.074	.078	.079	May
	.022	.031	.040	.063	.067	.070	.068	.070	.070	.072	.075	.077	Jun
	.024	.032	.042	.064	.069	.071	.069	.072	.071	.073	.077	.078	Jul
	.014	.022	.032	.054	.059	.061	.059	.062	.061	.063	.067	.068	Aug
	.012	.020	.030	.052	.057	.059	.057	.060	.059	.061	.064	.066	Sep
	.006	.014	.023	.045	.050	.052	.050	.053	.053	.054	.058	.059	Oct
	.003	.011	.020	.042	.047	.049	.047	.050	.049	.051	.055	.056	Nov
	.004	.012	.021	.043	.048	.050	.048	.051	.050	.052	.056	.057	Dec
		.008	.018	.039	.044	.046	.044	.047	.046	.048	.052	.053	**1985** Jan
			.009	.031	.036	.038	.036	.039	.038	.040	.043	.045	Feb
				.021	.026	.028	.026	.029	.028	.030	.034	.035	Mar
					.005	.007	.005	.007	.007	.009	.012	.013	Apr
						.002	.000	.003	.002	.004	.007	.009	May
							.000	.001	.000	.002	.005	.007	Jun
								.003	.002	.004	.007	.009	Jul
									.000	.001	.005	.006	Aug
										.002	.005	.006	Sep
											.003	.005	Oct
												.001	Nov
													Dec

Table of indexation factors RD

RI	1986 Jan	Feb	Mar	Apr	May	Jun	Jul	Aug	Sep	Oct	Nov	Dec	1987 Jan	Feb	Mar	Apr	May	Jun	Jul	Aug	Sep	Oct	Nov	Dec
1982																								
Mar	.212	.216	.218	.229	.232	.231	.228	.231	.237	.239	.250	.254	.259	.264	.266	.281	.283	.283	.281	.285	.289	.295	.302	.300
Apr	.188	.192	.194	.205	.207	.207	.203	.207	.213	.215	.225	.229	.234	.239	.241	.256	.257	.257	.256	.260	.264	.270	.276	.275
May	.179	.184	.185	.197	.199	.198	.195	.198	.204	.206	.216	.220	.225	.230	.233	.247	.248	.248	.247	.251	.255	.261	.267	.266
Jun	.176	.180	.182	.193	.195	.195	.191	.195	.201	.203	.213	.217	.222	.227	.229	.244	.245	.245	.244	.247	.251	.257	.263	.262
Jul	.176	.180	.181	.193	.195	.194	.191	.195	.201	.202	.213	.217	.221	.226	.229	.243	.245	.245	.243	.247	.251	.257	.263	.262
Aug	.175	.180	.181	.193	.195	.194	.191	.194	.200	.202	.212	.216	.221	.226	.228	.243	.244	.244	.243	.247	.250	.256	.262	.261
Sep	.176	.180	.182	.193	.195	.195	.191	.195	.201	.203	.213	.217	.222	.227	.229	.244	.245	.245	.244	.247	.251	.257	.263	.262
Oct	.170	.174	.176	.187	.190	.189	.186	.189	.195	.197	.207	.211	.216	.221	.223	.238	.239	.239	.238	.241	.245	.251	.257	.256
Nov	.164	.169	.170	.182	.184	.183	.180	.183	.189	.191	.201	.205	.210	.215	.217	.232	.233	.233	.232	.235	.239	.245	.251	.250
Dec	.167	.171	.172	.184	.186	.185	.182	.186	.191	.193	.203	.207	.212	.217	.219	.234	.235	.235	.234	.237	.241	.247	.253	.252
1983																								
Jan	.165	.169	.171	.182	.184	.184	.180	.184	.190	.192	.202	.206	.210	.215	.218	.232	.233	.233	.232	.236	.240	.246	.252	.250
Feb	.160	.164	.166	.177	.179	.179	.175	.179	.185	.187	.197	.201	.205	.210	.213	.227	.228	.228	.227	.231	.234	.240	.246	.245
Mar	.158	.162	.164	.175	.177	.177	.173	.177	.183	.185	.195	.199	.203	.208	.210	.225	.226	.226	.225	.228	.232	.238	.244	.243
Apr	.142	.146	.148	.159	.161	.160	.157	.161	.166	.168	.178	.182	.186	.191	.194	.208	.209	.209	.208	.211	.215	.221	.227	.226
May	.137	.141	.143	.154	.156	.155	.152	.156	.161	.163	.173	.177	.181	.186	.189	.203	.204	.204	.203	.206	.210	.216	.222	.220
Jun	.134	.139	.140	.151	.153	.153	.149	.153	.159	.160	.170	.174	.179	.183	.186	.200	.201	.201	.200	.203	.207	.213	.219	.218
Jul	.128	.133	.134	.145	.147	.147	.143	.147	.152	.154	.164	.168	.172	.177	.179	.193	.195	.195	.193	.197	.200	.206	.212	.211
Aug	.123	.128	.129	.140	.142	.141	.138	.142	.147	.149	.159	.163	.167	.172	.174	.188	.189	.189	.188	.192	.195	.201	.207	.206
Sep	.118	.123	.124	.135	.137	.136	.133	.137	.142	.144	.154	.158	.162	.167	.169	.183	.184	.184	.183	.186	.190	.196	.202	.200
Oct	.114	.119	.120	.131	.133	.132	.129	.133	.138	.140	.150	.154	.158	.163	.165	.179	.180	.180	.179	.182	.186	.191	.197	.196
Nov	.111	.115	.116	.127	.129	.128	.125	.129	.134	.136	.146	.149	.154	.158	.161	.175	.176	.176	.175	.178	.182	.187	.193	.192
Dec	.108	.112	.113	.124	.126	.125	.122	.126	.131	.133	.143	.146	.151	.155	.158	.172	.173	.173	.172	.175	.178	.184	.190	.189
1984																								
Jan	.108	.112	.114	.125	.127	.126	.123	.126	.132	.134	.143	.147	.151	.156	.158	.172	.173	.173	.172	.176	.179	.185	.191	.189
Feb	.104	.108	.109	.120	.122	.122	.118	.122	.127	.129	.139	.142	.147	.151	.154	.167	.169	.169	.167	.171	.174	.180	.186	.185
Mar	.100	.104	.106	.116	.119	.118	.115	.118	.124	.125	.135	.139	.143	.148	.150	.164	.165	.165	.164	.167	.171	.176	.182	.181
Apr	.086	.090	.091	.102	.104	.103	.100	.104	.109	.111	.120	.124	.128	.133	.135	.148	.150	.150	.148	.152	.155	.161	.166	.165
May	.082	.086	.087	.098	.100	.099	.096	.099	.105	.107	.116	.120	.124	.128	.131	.144	.145	.145	.144	.148	.151	.157	.162	.161
Jun	.079	.083	.084	.095	.097	.096	.093	.097	.102	.104	.113	.117	.121	.126	.128	.141	.142	.142	.141	.145	.148	.154	.159	.158
Jul	.080	.084	.086	.096	.098	.098	.094	.098	.103	.105	.114	.118	.122	.127	.129	.143	.144	.144	.143	.146	.149	.155	.160	.159
Aug	.070	.074	.076	.086	.088	.087	.084	.088	.093	.095	.104	.108	.112	.116	.119	.132	.133	.133	.132	.135	.139	.144	.150	.149
Sep	.068	.072	.073	.084	.086	.085	.082	.086	.091	.093	.102	.105	.110	.114	.116	.130	.131	.131	.130	.133	.136	.142	.147	.146
Oct	.062	.065	.067	.077	.079	.079	.075	.079	.084	.086	.095	.099	.103	.107	.109	.123	.124	.124	.123	.126	.129	.135	.140	.139
Nov	.058	.062	.064	.074	.076	.075	.072	.076	.081	.082	.092	.095	.099	.104	.106	.119	.120	.120	.119	.123	.126	.131	.137	.136
Dec	.059	.063	.064	.075	.077	.076	.073	.076	.082	.083	.093	.096	.100	.105	.107	.120	.121	.121	.120	.124	.127	.132	.138	.137
1985																								
Jan	.055	.059	.061	.071	.073	.072	.069	.073	.078	.079	.089	.092	.096	.101	.103	.116	.117	.117	.116	.119	.123	.128	.134	.133
Feb	.047	.051	.052	.062	.064	.064	.061	.064	.069	.071	.080	.084	.088	.092	.094	.107	.108	.108	.107	.111	.114	.119	.125	.124
Mar	.037	.041	.042	.052	.054	.054	.051	.054	.059	.061	.070	.073	.078	.082	.084	.097	.098	.098	.097	.100	.103	.109	.114	.113
Apr	.016	.019	.021	.030	.032	.032	.029	.032	.037	.039	.048	.051	.055	.059	.061	.074	.075	.075	.074	.077	.080	.086	.091	.090
May	.011	.015	.016	.026	.028	.027	.024	.027	.032	.034	.043	.046	.050	.055	.057	.069	.070	.070	.069	.072	.076	.081	.086	.085
Jun	.009	.012	.014	.024	.026	.025	.022	.025	.030	.032	.041	.044	.048	.052	.054	.067	.068	.068	.067	.070	.073	.078	.084	.083
Jul	.011	.014	.016	.026	.027	.027	.024	.027	.032	.034	.043	.046	.050	.054	.056	.069	.070	.070	.069	.072	.075	.080	.086	.085
Aug	.008	.012	.013	.023	.025	.024	.021	.024	.029	.031	.040	.043	.047	.051	.054	.066	.067	.067	.066	.069	.072	.078	.083	.082
Sep	.008	.012	.014	.023	.025	.025	.022	.025	.030	.032	.040	.044	.048	.052	.054	.067	.068	.068	.067	.070	.073	.078	.083	.082
Oct	.007	.011	.012	.022	.024	.023	.020	.023	.028	.030	.039	.042	.046	.050	.052	.065	.066	.066	.065	.068	.071	.076	.082	.081
Nov	.003	.007	.008	.018	.020	.020	.017	.020	.025	.026	.035	.039	.043	.047	.049	.061	.062	.062	.061	.064	.068	.073	.078	.077
Dec	.002	.006	.007	.017	.019	.018	.015	.018	.023	.025	.034	.037	.041	.045	.047	.060	.061	.061	.060	.063	.066	.071	.077	.076
1986																								
Jan		.004	.005	.015	.017	.016	.013	.016	.021	.023	.032	.035	.039	.043	.045	.058	.059	.059	.058	.061	.064	.069	.074	.073
Feb			.001	.011	.013	.012	.009	.013	.018	.019	.028	.031	.035	.039	.041	.054	.055	.055	.054	.057	.060	.065	.070	.069
Mar				.010	.012	.011	.008	.011	.016	.018	.026	.030	.034	.038	.040	.052	.053	.053	.052	.056	.059	.064	.069	.068
Apr					.002	.001	.000	.002	.006	.008	.017	.020	.024	.028	.030	.042	.043	.043	.042	.045	.048	.054	.059	.058
May						.000	.000	.000	.005	.006	.015	.018	.022	.026	.028	.040	.041	.041	.040	.043	.047	.052	.057	.056
Jun							.000	.000	.005	.007	.015	.019	.023	.027	.029	.041	.042	.042	.041	.044	.047	.052	.057	.056
Jul								.003	.008	.010	.018	.022	.025	.030	.032	.044	.045	.045	.044	.047	.050	.055	.060	.059
Aug									.005	.006	.015	.018	.022	.026	.028	.041	.042	.042	.041	.044	.047	.052	.057	.056
Sep										.002	.010	.013	.017	.021	.023	.036	.037	.037	.036	.039	.042	.047	.052	.051
Oct											.008	.012	.016	.020	.022	.034	.035	.035	.034	.037	.040	.045	.050	.049
Nov												.003	.007	.011	.013	.025	.026	.026	.025	.028	.031	.036	.041	.040
Dec													.004	.008	.010	.022	.023	.023	.022	.025	.028	.033	.038	.037
1987																								
Jan														.004	.006	.018	.019	.019	.018	.021	.024	.029	.034	.033
Feb															.002	.014	.015	.015	.014	.017	.020	.025	.030	.029
Mar																.012	.013	.013	.012	.015	.018	.023	.028	.027
Apr																	.001	.001	.000	.003	.006	.011	.016	.015
May																		.000	.000	.002	.005	.010	.015	.014
Jun																			.000	.002	.005	.010	.015	.014
Jul																				.003	.006	.011	.016	.015
Aug																					.003	.008	.013	.012
Sep																						.005	.010	.009
Oct																							.005	.004
Nov																								.000
Dec																								

14

Table of indexation factors

1988

	Jan	Feb	Mar	Apr	May	Jun	Jul	Aug	Sep	Oct	Nov	Dec
1982 Mar	.300	.305	.310	.332	.337	.342	.343	.358	.365	.378	.385	.388
Apr	.275	.280	.285	.306	.310	.315	.317	.331	.338	.351	.357	.361
May	.266	.270	.275	.296	.301	.306	.307	.322	.328	.342	.348	.351
Jun	.262	.267	.272	.293	.297	.302	.304	.318	.324	.338	.344	.348
Jul	.262	.267	.271	.292	.297	.302	.303	.318	.324	.337	.343	.347
Aug	.261	.266	.271	.292	.297	.302	.303	.317	.324	.337	.343	.347
Sep	.262	.267	.272	.293	.297	.302	.304	.318	.324	.338	.344	.348
Oct	.256	.261	.266	.286	.291	.296	.297	.312	.318	.331	.337	.341
Nov	250	.255	.259	.280	.285	.290	.291	.305	.311	.325	.331	.334
Dec	.252	.257	.262	.282	.287	.292	.293	.308	.314	.327	.333	.337
1983 Jan	.250	.255	.260	.281	.286	.290	.292	.306	.312	.325	.332	.335
Feb	.245	.250	.255	.275	.280	.285	.286	.301	.307	.320	.326	.329
Mar	.243	.248	.252	.273	.278	.283	.284	.298	.304	.317	.323	.327
Apr	.226	.230	.235	.255	.260	.265	.266	.280	.286	.299	.305	.309
May	.220	.225	.230	.250	.255	.259	.261	.275	.281	.294	.300	.303
Jun	.218	.222	.227	.247	.252	.256	.258	.272	.278	.291	.297	.300
Jul	.211	.216	.220	.240	.245	.250	.251	.265	.271	.284	.290	.293
Aug	.206	.210	.215	.235	.240	.244	.245	.259	.265	.278	.284	.287
Sep	.200	.205	.210	.229	.234	.239	.240	.254	.260	.272	.278	.282
Oct	.196	.201	.205	.225	.230	.234	.235	.249	.255	.268	.274	.277
Nov	.192	.197	.201	.221	.225	.230	.231	.245	.251	.263	.269	.273
Dec	.189	.193	.198	.218	.222	.227	.228	.242	.247	.260	.266	.269
1984 Jan	.189	.194	.199	.218	.223	.227	.229	.242	.248	.261	.267	.270
Feb	.185	.189	.194	.213	.218	.222	.224	.237	.243	.256	.261	.265
Mar	.181	.185	.190	.209	.214	.219	.220	.233	.239	.252	.257	.261
Apr	.165	.170	.174	.194	.198	.203	.204	.217	.223	.235	.241	.244
May	.161	.166	.170	.189	.194	.198	.199	.213	.218	.231	.236	.240
Jun	.158	.163	.167	.186	.191	.195	.196	.210	.215	.228	.233	.237
Jul	.159	.164	.168	.187	.192	.196	.198	.211	.217	.229	.235	.238
Aug	.149	.153	.157	.176	.181	.185	.186	.200	.205	.218	.223	.226
Sep	.146	.151	.155	.174	.179	.183	.184	.197	.203	.215	.221	.224
Oct	.139	.144	.148	.167	.171	.176	.177	.190	.196	.208	.213	.216
Nov	.136	.140	.145	.163	.168	.172	.173	.186	.192	.204	.209	.213
Dec	.137	.141	.146	.164	.169	.173	.174	.187	.193	.205	.210	.214
1985 Jan	.133	.137	.141	.160	.164	.169	.170	.183	.189	.201	.206	.209
Feb	.124	.128	.132	.151	.155	.159	.161	.174	.179	.191	.196	.200
Mar	.113	.117	.122	.140	.144	.149	.150	.163	.168	.180	.185	.189
Apr	.090	.094	.098	.116	.121	.125	.126	.138	.144	.155	.161	.164
May	.085	.089	.093	.111	.115	.120	.121	.133	.139	.150	.155	.159
Jun	.083	.087	.091	.109	.113	.117	.118	.131	.136	.148	.153	.156
Jul	.085	.089	.093	.111	.115	.119	.120	.133	.138	.150	.155	.158
Aug	.082	.086	.090	.108	.112	.116	.117	.130	.135	.147	.152	.155
Sep	.082	.087	.091	.109	.113	.117	.118	.131	.136	.147	.153	.156
Oct	.081	.085	.089	.107	.111	.115	.116	.129	.134	.146	.151	.154
Nov	.077	.081	.085	.103	.107	.111	.112	.125	.130	.142	.147	.150
Dec	.076	.080	.084	.102	.106	.110	.111	.123	.129	.140	.145	.148
1986 Jan	.073	.077	.082	.099	.103	.108	.109	.121	.126	.138	.143	.146
Feb	.069	.073	.078	.095	.099	.103	.105	.117	.122	.134	.139	.142
Mar	.068	.072	.076	.094	.098	.102	.103	.115	.121	.132	.137	.140
Apr	.058	.062	.066	.083	.087	.091	.092	.105	.110	.121	.126	.129
May	.056	.060	.064	.081	.085	.089	.090	.103	.108	.119	.124	.127
Jun	.056	.060	.064	.082	.086	.090	.091	.103	.108	.120	.125	.128
Jul	.059	.063	.068	.085	.089	.093	.094	.106	.112	.123	.128	.131
Aug	.056	.060	.064	.082	.086	.090	.091	.103	.108	.119	.125	.128
Sep	.051	.055	.059	.076	.080	.084	.085	.098	.103	.114	.119	.122
Oct	.049	.053	.057	.075	.079	.083	.084	.096	.101	.112	.117	.120
Nov	.040	.044	.048	.066	.070	.074	.075	.087	.092	.103	.108	.111
Dec	.037	.041	.045	.062	.066	.070	.071	.083	.088	.099	.104	.107
1987 Jan	.033	.037	.041	.058	.062	.066	.067	.079	.084	.095	.100	.103
Feb	.029	.033	.037	.054	.058	.062	.063	.075	.080	.091	.096	.099
Mar	.027	.031	.035	.052	.056	.060	.061	.073	.078	.088	.093	.096
Apr	.015	.019	.023	.039	.043	.047	.048	.060	.065	.076	.081	.083
May	.014	.018	.022	.038	.042	.046	.047	.059	.064	.075	.079	.082
Jun	.014	.018	.022	.038	.042	.046	.047	.059	.064	.075	.079	.082
Jul	.015	.019	.023	.039	.043	.047	.048	.060	.065	.076	.081	.083
Aug	.012	.016	.020	.036	.040	.044	.045	.057	.062	.072	.077	.080
Sep	.009	.013	.017	.033	.037	.041	.042	.054	.059	.069	.074	.077
Oct	.004	.008	.012	.028	.032	.036	.037	.049	.053	.064	.069	.072
Nov	.000	.003	.007	.023	.027	.031	.032	.044	.048	.059	.064	.067
Dec	.000	.004	.008	.024	.028	.032	.033	.045	.049	.060	.065	.068

1989

	Jan	Feb	Mar	Apr	May	Jun	Jul	Aug	Sep	Oct	Nov	Dec
1982 Mar	.397	.407	.414	.439	.448	.453	.454	.458	.468	.479	.492	.495
Apr	.370	.380	.386	.410	.419	.424	.425	.429	.439	.450	.462	.466
May	.360	.370	.376	.400	.409	.414	.415	.419	.429	.440	.452	.455
Jun	.356	.366	.372	.396	.405	.410	.411	.415	.425	.436	.448	.451
Jul	.356	.365	.372	.396	.405	.409	.411	.414	.424	.435	.447	.451
Aug	.355	.365	.371	.396	.404	.409	.410	.414	.424	.435	.447	.451
Sep	.356	.366	.372	.396	.405	.410	.411	.415	.425	.436	.448	.451
Oct	.349	.359	.365	.390	.398	.403	.404	.408	.418	.428	.441	.444
Nov	.343	.353	.359	.383	.391	.396	.397	.401	.411	.421	.434	.437
Dec	.345	.355	.361	.385	.394	.399	.400	.403	.413	.424	.436	.440
1983 Jan	.344	.353	.359	.384	.392	.397	.398	.402	.411	.422	.434	.438
Feb	.338	.348	.354	.378	.386	.391	.392	.396	.405	.416	.428	.432
Mar	.335	.345	.351	.375	.384	.388	.390	.393	.403	.414	.426	.429
Apr	.317	.326	.332	.356	.364	.369	.370	.374	.383	.394	.406	.410
May	.311	.321	.327	.350	.359	.363	.365	.368	.378	.388	.400	.404
Jun	.308	.318	.324	.347	.355	.360	.361	.365	.374	.385	.397	.400
Jul	.301	.311	.317	.340	.348	.353	.354	.358	.367	.378	.389	.393
Aug	.296	.305	.311	.334	.342	.347	.348	.352	.361	.371	.383	.387
Sep	.290	.299	.305	.328	.336	.341	.342	.346	.355	.365	.377	.380
Oct	.285	.295	.300	.323	.332	.336	.337	.341	.350	.361	.372	.376
Nov	.281	.290	.296	.319	.327	.332	.333	.336	.345	.356	.367	.371
Dec	.277	.287	.292	.315	.323	.328	.329	.333	.342	.352	.364	.367
1984 Jan	.278	.287	.293	.316	.324	.329	.330	.333	.343	.353	.365	.368
Feb	.273	.282	.288	.311	.319	.323	.325	.328	.337	.347	.359	.362
Mar	.269	.278	.284	.307	.315	.319	.320	.324	.333	.343	.355	.358
Apr	.252	.261	.267	.289	.297	.302	.303	.306	.315	.326	.337	.340
May	.248	.257	.262	.285	.293	.297	.298	.302	.311	.321	.332	.335
Jun	.244	.253	.259	.281	.289	.294	.295	.298	.307	.317	.328	.332
Jul	.246	.255	.260	.283	.291	.295	.296	.300	.309	.319	.330	.333
Aug	.234	.243	.249	.271	.279	.283	.284	.288	.296	.306	.318	.321
Sep	.232	.241	.246	.268	.276	.281	.282	.285	.294	.304	.315	.318
Oct	.224	.233	.239	.261	.268	.273	.274	.277	.286	.296	.307	.310
Nov	.220	.229	.235	.257	.264	.269	.270	.273	.282	.292	.303	.306
Dec	.221	.230	.236	.258	.265	.270	.271	.274	.283	.293	.304	.307
1985 Jan	.217	.226	.231	.253	.261	.265	.266	.270	.278	.288	.299	.303
Feb	.207	.216	.221	.243	.251	.255	.256	.260	.268	.278	.289	.292
Mar	.196	.205	.210	.232	.239	.244	.245	.248	.256	.266	.277	.280
Apr	.171	.180	.185	.206	.213	.218	.219	.222	.230	.240	.250	.253
May	.166	.174	.180	.201	.208	.212	.213	.216	.225	.234	.245	.248
Jun	.163	.172	.177	.198	.205	.209	.211	.214	.222	.232	.242	.245
Jul	.166	.174	.179	.200	.208	.212	.213	.216	.224	.234	.244	.247
Aug	.162	.171	.176	.197	.204	.209	.210	.213	.221	.231	.241	.244
Sep	.163	.171	.177	.198	.205	.209	.210	.213	.222	.231	.242	.245
Oct	.161	.170	.175	.196	.203	.207	.208	.211	.220	.229	.240	.243
Nov	.157	.166	.171	.192	.199	.203	.204	.207	.216	.225	.235	.239
Dec	.156	.164	.169	.190	.197	.202	.203	.206	.214	.223	.234	.237
1986 Jan	.153	.162	.167	.188	.195	.199	.200	.203	.211	.221	.231	.234
Feb	.149	.157	.162	.183	.190	.195	.196	.199	.207	.216	.227	.230
Mar	.148	.156	.161	.182	.189	.193	.194	.197	.205	.215	.225	.228
Apr	.137	.145	.150	.170	.177	.182	.183	.186	.194	.203	.213	.216
May	.134	.143	.148	.168	.175	.179	.180	.184	.192	.201	.211	.214
Jun	.135	.143	.148	.169	.176	.180	.181	.184	.192	.201	.212	.215
Jul	.138	.146	.152	.172	.179	.183	.184	.187	.196	.205	.215	.218
Aug	.135	.143	.148	.168	.176	.180	.181	.184	.192	.201	.211	.214
Sep	.129	.137	.142	.163	.170	.174	.175	.178	.186	.195	.205	.209
Oct	.127	.136	.141	.161	.168	.172	.173	.176	.184	.193	.204	.207
Nov	.118	.126	.131	.151	.158	.162	.163	.166	.174	.183	.193	.196
Dec	.114	.122	.127	.147	.154	.158	.159	.162	.170	.179	.190	.193
1987 Jan	.110	.118	.123	.143	.150	.154	.155	.158	.166	.175	.185	.188
Feb	.106	.114	.119	.138	.145	.149	.150	.153	.161	.170	.180	.183
Mar	.103	.111	.116	.136	.143	.147	.148	.151	.159	.168	.178	.181
Apr	.090	.098	.103	.123	.130	.134	.135	.138	.145	.154	.164	.167
May	.089	.097	.102	.122	.129	.132	.133	.136	.144	.153	.163	.166
Jun	.089	.097	.102	.122	.129	.132	.133	.136	.144	.153	.163	.166
Jul	.090	.098	.103	.123	.130	.134	.135	.138	.145	.154	.164	.167
Aug	.087	.095	.100	.119	.126	.130	.131	.134	.142	.151	.161	.164
Sep	.084	.092	.097	.116	.123	.127	.128	.131	.139	.147	.157	.160
Oct	.079	.086	.091	.111	.118	.121	.122	.125	.133	.142	.152	.155
Nov	.074	.081	.086	.105	.112	.116	.117	.120	.128	.136	.146	.149
Dec	.075	.082	.087	.106	.113	.117	.118	.121	.129	.137	.147	.150

Table of indexation factors **RD**

		1990												1991												1992	
RI	**1982**	Jan	Feb	Mar	Apr	May	Jun	Jul	Aug	Sep	Oct	Nov	Dec	Jan	Feb	Mar	Apr	May	Jun	Jul	Aug	Sep	Oct	Nov	Dec	Jan	Feb
	Mar	.504	.513	.528	.575	.589	.595	.596	.612	.628	.640	.636	.635	.639	.648	.654	.675	.680	.688	.684	.688	.694	.701	.707	.708	.707	.716
	Apr	.475	.483	.498	.544	.557	.563	.565	.581	.596	.608	.604	.603	.607	.615	.621	.642	.647	.655	.651	.655	.661	.667	.673	.674	.673	.682
	May	.464	.473	.487	.533	.546	.552	.553	.569	.584	.596	.593	.591	.595	.604	.610	.631	.636	.643	.639	.643	.649	.655	.661	.663	.661	.670
	Jun	.460	.469	.483	.528	.542	.548	.549	.565	.580	.592	.588	.587	.591	.599	.605	.626	.631	.638	.635	.638	.644	.651	.657	.658	.657	.665
	Jul	.460	.468	.483	.528	.541	.547	.549	.565	.579	.591	.588	.587	.590	.599	.605	.626	.631	.638	.634	.638	.644	.650	.656	.657	.656	.665
	Aug	.459	.468	.482	.527	.541	.547	.548	.564	.579	.591	.587	.586	.590	.598	.604	.625	.630	.637	.634	.637	.643	.650	.656	.657	.656	.664
	Sep	.460	.469	.483	.528	.542	.548	.549	.565	.580	.592	.588	.587	.591	.599	.605	.626	.631	.638	.635	.638	.644	.651	.657	.658	.657	.665
	Oct	.453	.461	.476	.521	.534	.540	.542	.557	.572	.584	.580	.579	.583	.591	.597	.618	.623	.630	.627	.630	.636	.642	.649	.650	.649	.657
	Nov	.446	.454	.469	.513	.527	.533	.534	.550	.564	.576	.573	.571	.575	.584	.590	.610	.615	.622	.619	.622	.628	.634	.640	.642	.640	.649
	Dec	.448	.457	.471	.516	.530	.536	.537	.553	.567	.579	.576	.574	.578	.586	.593	.613	.618	.625	.622	.625	.631	.637	.643	.645	.643	.652
	1983																										
	Jan	.447	.455	.470	.514	.528	.534	.535	.551	.565	.577	.574	.572	.576	.585	.591	.611	.616	.623	.620	.623	.629	.635	.641	.643	.641	.650
	Feb	.440	.449	.463	.508	.521	.527	.528	.544	.558	.571	.567	.566	.569	.578	.584	.604	.609	.616	.613	.616	.622	.628	.634	.636	.634	.643
	Mar	.438	.446	.461	.505	.518	.524	.526	.541	.556	.568	.564	.563	.566	.575	.581	.601	.606	.613	.610	.613	.619	.625	.631	.633	.631	.640
	Apr	.418	.426	.440	.484	.497	.503	.504	.520	.534	.546	.542	.541	.545	.553	.559	.579	.584	.591	.587	.591	.597	.603	.609	.610	.609	.617
	May	.412	.420	.434	.478	.491	.497	.498	.513	.528	.539	.536	.535	.538	.547	.552	.573	.577	.584	.581	.584	.590	.596	.602	.603	.602	.610
	Jun	.409	.417	.431	.475	.487	.493	.495	.510	.524	.536	.532	.531	.535	.543	.549	.569	.574	.581	.577	.581	.586	.592	.598	.599	.598	.607
	Jul	.401	.409	.423	.467	.480	.485	.487	.502	.516	.528	.524	.523	.526	.535	.540	.560	.565	.572	.569	.572	.578	.584	.590	.591	.590	.598
	Aug	.395	.403	.417	.460	.473	.479	.480	.495	.509	.521	.517	.516	.520	.528	.534	.553	.558	.565	.562	.565	.571	.577	.583	.584	.583	.591
	Sep	.389	.397	.411	.454	.466	.472	.473	.489	.502	.514	.511	.509	.513	.521	.527	.547	.551	.558	.555	.558	.564	.570	.576	.577	.576	.584
	Oct	.384	.392	.406	.449	.461	.467	.468	.483	.497	.509	.505	.504	.508	.516	.521	.541	.546	.553	.549	.553	.559	.564	.570	.571	.570	.578
	Nov	.379	.387	.401	.443	.456	.462	.463	.478	.492	.503	.500	.499	.502	.510	.516	.536	.540	.547	.544	.547	.553	.559	.565	.566	.565	.573
	Dec	.375	.383	.397	.440	.452	.458	.459	.474	.488	.500	.496	.495	.498	.506	.512	.532	.536	.543	.540	.543	.549	.555	.561	.562	.561	.569
	1984																										
	Jan	.376	.384	.398	.441	.453	.459	.460	.475	.489	.500	.497	.496	.499	.507	.513	.533	.537	.544	.541	.544	.550	.556	.561	.563	.561	.569
	Feb	.370	.378	.392	.435	.447	.453	.454	.469	.483	.494	.491	.490	.493	.501	.507	.526	.531	.538	.534	.538	.544	.549	.555	.556	.555	.563
	Mar	.366	.374	.388	.430	.443	.448	.450	.464	.478	.490	.486	.485	.488	.496	.502	.522	.526	.533	.530	.533	.539	.544	.550	.551	.550	.558
	Apr	.348	.356	.370	.411	.424	.429	.430	.445	.459	.470	.467	.465	.469	.477	.482	.502	.506	.513	.509	.513	.518	.524	.530	.531	.530	.538
	May	.343	.351	.364	.406	.418	.424	.425	.440	.453	.464	.461	.460	.463	.471	.477	.496	.500	.507	.504	.507	.513	.518	.524	.525	.524	.532
	Jun	.340	.348	.361	.402	.415	.420	.422	.436	.450	.461	.457	.456	.460	.467	.473	.492	.497	.503	.500	.503	.509	.515	.520	.521	.520	.528
	Jul	.341	.349	.363	.404	.416	.422	.423	.438	.451	.462	.459	.458	.461	.469	.475	.494	.498	.505	.502	.505	.511	.516	.522	.523	.522	.530
	Aug	.329	.336	.350	.391	.403	.409	.410	.424	.438	.449	.445	.444	.448	.455	.461	.480	.484	.491	.488	.491	.497	.502	.508	.509	.508	.516
	Sep	.326	.334	.347	.388	.400	.406	.407	.422	.435	.446	.443	.442	.445	.453	.458	.477	.481	.488	.485	.488	.494	.499	.505	.506	.505	.513
	Oct	.318	.326	.339	.380	.392	.397	.398	.413	.426	.437	.434	.433	.436	.444	.449	.468	.472	.479	.476	.479	.484	.490	.496	.497	.496	.503
	Nov	.314	.322	.335	.375	.388	.393	.394	.408	.422	.433	.429	.428	.432	.439	.445	.463	.468	.474	.471	.474	.480	.485	.491	.492	.491	.499
	Dec	.315	.323	.336	.377	.389	.394	.395	.410	.423	.434	.431	.429	.433	.440	.446	.465	.469	.476	.472	.476	.481	.487	.492	.493	.492	.500
	1985																										
	Jan	.310	.318	.331	.372	.384	.389	.390	.405	.418	.429	.425	.424	.428	.435	.441	.459	.464	.470	.467	.470	.476	.481	.487	.488	.487	.494
	Feb	.300	.307	.320	.361	.373	.378	.379	.393	.406	.417	.414	.413	.416	.424	.429	.448	.452	.459	.455	.459	.464	.469	.475	.476	.475	.483
	Mar	.288	.295	.308	.348	.360	.365	.366	.380	.393	.404	.401	.400	.403	.411	.416	.434	.439	.445	.442	.445	.450	.456	.461	.462	.461	.469
	Apr	.261	.268	.281	.320	.332	.337	.338	.352	.364	.375	.372	.371	.374	.381	.386	.404	.409	.415	.412	.415	.420	.425	.431	.432	.431	.438
	May	.255	.262	.275	.314	.326	.331	.332	.345	.358	.369	.365	.364	.368	.375	.380	.398	.402	.408	.405	.408	.414	.419	.424	.425	.424	.432
	Jun	.252	.260	.272	.311	.323	.328	.329	.343	.355	.366	.363	.361	.365	.372	.377	.395	.399	.405	.402	.405	.411	.416	.421	.422	.421	.429
	Jul	.255	.262	.275	.314	.325	.330	.331	.345	.358	.368	.365	.364	.367	.375	.380	.398	.402	.408	.405	.408	.413	.419	.424	.425	.424	.431
	Aug	.251	.259	.271	.310	.322	.327	.328	.342	.354	.365	.361	.360	.364	.371	.376	.394	.398	.404	.401	.404	.410	.415	.420	.421	.420	.427
	Sep	.252	.259	.272	.311	.322	.328	.329	.342	.355	.365	.362	.361	.364	.372	.377	.395	.399	.405	.402	.405	.410	.416	.421	.422	.421	.428
	Oct	.250	.257	.270	.309	.320	.325	.327	.340	.353	.363	.360	.359	.362	.369	.375	.392	.397	.403	.400	.403	.408	.413	.419	.420	.419	.426
	Nov	.246	.253	.266	.304	.316	.321	.322	.336	.348	.358	.355	.354	.357	.365	.370	.388	.392	.398	.395	.398	.403	.408	.414	.415	.414	.421
	Dec	.244	.251	.264	.303	.314	.319	.320	.334	.346	.357	.354	.352	.356	.363	.368	.386	.390	.396	.393	.396	.401	.407	.412	.413	.412	.419
	1986																										
	Jan	.242	.249	.261	.300	.311	.316	.317	.331	.343	.354	.351	.350	.353	.360	.365	.383	.387	.393	.390	.393	.398	.404	.409	.410	.409	.416
	Feb	.237	.244	.257	.295	.306	.312	.313	.326	.338	.349	.346	.345	.348	.355	.360	.378	.382	.388	.385	.388	.393	.399	.404	.405	.404	.411
	Mar	.235	.243	.255	.293	.305	.310	.311	.324	.337	.347	.344	.343	.346	.353	.358	.376	.380	.386	.383	.386	.392	.397	.402	.403	.402	.409
	Apr	.224	.231	.243	.281	.292	.297	.298	.312	.324	.334	.331	.330	.333	.340	.345	.363	.367	.373	.370	.373	.378	.383	.388	.389	.388	.396
	May	.221	.228	.241	.279	.290	.295	.296	.309	.321	.332	.329	.328	.331	.338	.343	.360	.364	.371	.367	.371	.376	.381	.386	.387	.386	.393
	Jun	.222	.229	.241	.279	.290	.296	.297	.310	.322	.332	.329	.328	.331	.339	.344	.361	.365	.371	.368	.371	.376	.381	.387	.388	.387	.394
	Jul	.225	.233	.245	.283	.294	.299	.300	.314	.326	.336	.333	.332	.335	.342	.347	.365	.369	.375	.372	.375	.380	.385	.391	.392	.391	.398
	Aug	.222	.229	.241	.279	.290	.295	.296	.310	.322	.332	.329	.328	.331	.338	.343	.361	.365	.371	.368	.371	.376	.381	.386	.387	.386	.393
	Sep	.216	.223	.235	.273	.284	.289	.290	.303	.315	.326	.322	.321	.324	.332	.337	.354	.358	.364	.361	.364	.369	.374	.379	.380	.379	.387
	Oct	.214	.221	.233	.271	.282	.287	.288	.301	.313	.323	.320	.319	.322	.330	.335	.352	.356	.362	.359	.362	.367	.372	.377	.378	.377	.384
	Nov	.204	.211	.223	.260	.271	.276	.277	.290	.302	.312	.309	.308	.311	.318	.323	.341	.345	.351	.348	.351	.356	.361	.366	.367	.366	.373
	Dec	.200	.207	.219	.256	.267	.272	.273	.286	.298	.308	.305	.304	.307	.314	.319	.336	.340	.346	.343	.346	.351	.356	.361	.362	.361	.368
	1987																										
	Jan	.195	.202	.214	.251	.262	.267	.268	.281	.293	.303	.300	.299	.302	.309	.314	.331	.335	.341	.338	.341	.346	.351	.356	.357	.356	.363
	Feb	.190	.197	.209	.246	.257	.262	.263	.276	.288	.298	.295	.294	.297	.304	.309	.326	.330	.336	.333	.336	.341	.346	.351	.352	.351	.358
	Mar	.188	.195	.207	.244	.254	.259	.260	.273	.285	.295	.292	.291	.294	.301	.306	.323	.327	.333	.330	.333	.338	.343	.348	.349	.348	.355
	Apr	.174	.181	.193	.229	.240	.245	.246	.258	.270	.280	.277	.276	.279	.286	.291	.307	.311	.317	.314	.317	.322	.327	.332	.333	.332	.339
	May	.173	.180	.191	.228	.238	.243	.244	.257	.269	.279	.276	.275	.278	.285	.289	.306	.310	.316	.313	.316	.321	.326	.331	.332	.331	.338
	Jun	.173	.180	.191	.228	.238	.243	.244	.257	.269	.279	.276	.275	.278	.285	.289	.306	.310	.316	.313	.316	.321	.326	.331	.332	.331	.338
	Jul	.174	.181	.193	.229	.240	.245	.246	.258	.270	.280	.277	.276	.279	.286	.291	.307	.311	.317	.314	.317	.322	.327	.332	.333	.332	.339
	Aug	.170	.177	.189	.225	.236	.241	.242	.255	.266	.276	.273	.272	.275	.282	.287	.304	.308	.313	.310	.313	.318	.323	.328	.329	.328	.335
	Sep	.167	.174	.186	.222	.232	.237	.238	.251	.263	.272	.270	.269	.271	.278	.283	.300	.304	.310	.307	.310	.314	.319	.324	.325	.324	.331
	Oct	.161	.168	.180	.216	.226	.231	.232	.245	.257	.266	.263	.262	.265	.272	.277	.293	.297	.303	.300	.303	.308	.313	.318	.319	.318	.325
	Nov	.156	.162	.174	.210	.221	.225	.226	.239	.250	.260	.257	.256	.259	.266	.271	.287	.291	.297	.294	.297	.302	.307	.311	.312	.311	.318
	Dec	.157	.164	.175	.211	.222	.227	.227	.240	.252	.261	.258	.258	.260	.267	.272	.288	.292	.298	.295	.298	.303	.308	.313	.314	.313	.319

Table of indexation factors

1988

Jan	Feb	Mar	Apr	May	Jun	Jul	Aug	Sep	Oct	Nov	Dec
	.004	.008	.024	.028	.032	.033	.045	.049	.060	.065	.068
		.004	.020	.024	.028	.029	.041	.045	.056	.061	.064
			.016	.020	.024	.025	,037	.041	.052	.057	.060
				.004	.008	.009	.020	.025	.035	.040	.043
					.004	.005	.016	.021	.031	.036	.039
						.001	.012	.017	.027	.032	.035
							.011	.016	.026	.031	.034
								.005	.015	.019	.022
									.010	.015	.018
										.005	.007
											.003

continuation from page 15

1989

Jan	Feb	Mar	Apr	May	Jun	Jul	Aug	Sep	Oct	Nov	Dec		
.075	.082	.087	.106	.113	.117	.118	.121	.129	.137	.147	.150		**1988** Jan
.070	.078	.083	.102	.109	.113	.114	.117	.124	.133	.143	.146		Feb
.066	.074	.079	.098	.105	.109	.110	.112	.120	.129	.138	.141		Mar
.049	.057	.061	.080	.087	.091	.092	.095	.102	.111	.120	.123		Apr
.045	.053	.057	.076	.083	.087	.088	.090	.098	.106	.116	.119		May
.041	.049	.053	.072	.079	.083	.083	.086	.094	.102	.112	.114		Jun
.040	.048	.052	.071	.078	.082	.082	.085	.093	.101	.111	.113		Jul
.029	.036	.041	.059	.066	.070	.070	.073	.081	.089	.098	.101		Aug
.024	.031	.036	.054	.061	.065	.065	.068	.076	.084	.093	.096		Sep
.014	.021	.026	.044	.050	.054	.055	.058	.065	.073	.082	.085		Oct
.009	.016	.021	.039	.045	.049	.050	.053	.060	.068	.077	.080		Nov
.006	.014	.018	.036	.043	.046	.047	.050	.057	.065	.074	.077		Dec
	.007	.012	.030	.036	.040	.041	.043	.050	.059	.068	.070		**1989** Jan
		.004	.022	.029	.032	.033	.036	.043	.051	.060	.063		Feb
			.018	.024	.028	.028	.031	.038	.046	.055	.058		Mar
				.006	.010	.010	.013	.020	.028	.037	.039		Apr
					.003	.004	.007	.014	.022	.030	.033		May
						.001	.003	.010	.018	.027	.029		Jun
							.003	.010	.017	.026	.029		Jul
								.007	.015	.023	.026		Aug
									.008	.016	.019		Sep
										.009	.011		Oct
											.003		Nov
													Dec

1990

Jan	Feb	Mar	Apr	May	Jun	Jul	Aug	Sep	Oct	Nov	Dec
.157	.164	.175	.211	.222	.227	.227	.240	.252	.261	.258	.258
.152	.159	.171	.206	.217	.222	.223	.235	.247	.257	.254	.253
.148	.155	.166	.202	.212	.217	.218	.231	.242	.252	.249	.248
.129	.136	.147	.182	.193	.198	.198	.211	.222	.232	.229	.228
.125	.132	.143	.178	.188	.193	.194	.206	.218	.227	.224	.223
.121	.128	.139	.174	.184	.189	.189	.202	.213	.222	.220	.219
.120	.127	.138	.172	.183	.187	.188	.201	.212	.221	.218	.217
.108	.114	.125	.159	.170	.174	.175	.187	.198	.208	.205	.204
.102	.109	.120	.154	.164	.169	.170	.182	.193	.202	.199	.198
.091	.098	.109	.142	.153	.157	.158	.170	.181	.190	.187	.186
.086	.093	.104	.137	.147	.152	.153	.165	.175	.185	.182	.181
.083	.090	.101	.134	.144	.149	.150	.161	.172	.181	.179	.178
.077	.083	.094	.127	.137	.141	.142	.154	.165	.174	.171	.170
.069	.075	.086	.119	.129	.133	.134	.146	.157	.165	.163	.162
.064	.070	.081	.114	.124	.128	.129	.141	.151	.160	.158	.157
.045	.052	.062	.094	.104	.108	.109	.121	.131	.140	.137	.136
.039	.045	.056	.088	.097	.102	.103	.114	.124	.133	.130	.130
.036	.042	.052	.084	.094	.098	.099	.110	.120	.129	.127	.126
.035	.041	.051	.083	.093	.097	.098	.109	.119	.128	.126	.125
.032	.038	.048	.080	.090	.094	.095	.106	.117	.125	.123	.122
.025	.031	.041	.073	.082	.087	.087	.099	.109	.117	.115	.114
.017	.023	.033	.065	.074	.078	.079	.090	.100	.109	.106	.106
.008	.014	.024	.056	.065	.069	.070	.081	.091	.100	.097	.096
.006	.012	.022	.053	.062	.066	.067	.078	.088	.097	.094	.093
	.006	.016	.047	.056	.060	.061	.072	.082	.090	.088	.087
		.010	.041	.050	.054	.055	.066	.076	.084	.082	.081
			.030	.040	.044	.044	.055	.065	.073	.071	.070
				.009	.013	.014	.024	.034	.042	.039	.038
					.004	.005	.015	.025	.032	.030	.029
						.001	.011	.021	.028	.026	.025
							.010	.020	.028	.025	.024
								.009	.017	.015	.014
									.008	.005	.005
										.000	.000
											.000

continuation from page 16

1991 / 1992

1991 Jan	Feb	Mar	Apr	May	Jun	Jul	Aug	Sep	Oct	Nov	Dec	1992 Jan	Feb	
.260	.267	.272	.288	.292	.298	.295	.298	.303	.308	.313	.314	.313	.319	**1988** Jan
.256	.262	.267	.284	.287	.293	.290	.293	.298	.303	.308	.309	.308	.314	Feb
.251	.257	.262	.279	.282	.288	.285	.288	.293	.298	.303	.304	.303	.309	Mar
.231	.237	.242	.258	.262	.267	.265	.267	.272	.277	.282	.283	.282	.288	Apr
.226	.233	.237	.253	.257	.263	.260	.263	.267	.272	.277	.278	.277	.283	May
.221	.228	.233	.249	.252	.258	.255	.258	.263	.267	.272	.273	.272	.279	Jun
.220	.227	.231	.247	.251	.257	.254	.257	.261	.266	.271	.272	.271	.277	Jul
.207	.213	.218	.234	.237	.243	.240	.243	.247	.252	.257	.258	.257	.263	Aug
.201	.208	.212	.228	.232	.237	.234	.237	.242	.246	.251	.252	.251	.257	Sep
.189	.195	.200	.216	.219	.225	.222	.225	.229	.234	.238	.239	.238	.245	Oct
.184	.190	.195	.210	.214	.219	.216	.219	.224	.228	.233	.234	.233	.239	Nov
.180	.187	.191	.207	.210	.216	.213	.216	.220	.225	.229	.230	.229	.236	Dec
.173	.179	.184	.199	.203	.208	.205	.208	.213	.217	.222	.223	.222	.228	**1989** Jan
.165	.171	.175	.191	.194	.199	.197	.199	.204	.208	.213	.214	.213	.219	Feb
.159	.166	.170	.185	.189	.194	.191	.194	.199	.203	.207	.208	.207	.214	Mar
.139	.145	.150	.164	.168	.173	.171	.173	.178	.182	.186	.187	.186	.192	Apr
.132	.138	.143	.157	.161	.166	.163	.166	.170	.175	.179	.180	.179	.185	May
.128	.134	.139	.153	.157	.162	.159	.162	.166	.171	.175	.176	.175	.181	Jun
.127	.133	.138	.152	.156	.161	.158	.161	.165	.170	.174	.175	.174	.180	Jul
.124	.130	.135	.149	.153	.158	.155	.158	.162	.167	.171	.172	.171	.177	Aug
.117	.123	.127	.142	.145	.150	.148	.150	.154	.159	.163	.164	.163	.169	Sep
.108	.114	.118	.133	.136	.141	.139	.141	.146	.150	.154	.155	.154	.160	Oct
.099	.105	.109	.123	.127	.132	.129	.132	.136	.140	.144	.145	.144	.150	Nov
.096	.102	.106	.120	.124	.129	.126	.129	.133	.137	.141	.142	.141	.147	Dec
.090	.095	.100	.114	.117	.122	.120	.122	.126	.131	.135	.136	.135	.141	**1990** Jan
.083	.089	.093	.107	.111	.116	.113	.116	.120	.124	.128	.129	.128	.134	Feb
.072	.078	.082	.096	.100	.105	.102	.105	.109	.113	.117	.118	.117	.123	Mar
.041	.046	.050	.064	.067	.072	.070	.072	.076	.080	.084	.085	.084	.090	Apr
.032	.037	.041	.055	.058	.063	.060	.063	.067	.071	.074	.075	.074	.080	May
.028	.033	.037	.051	.054	.058	.056	.058	.062	.066	.070	.071	.070	.076	Jun
.027	.032	.036	.050	.053	.058	.055	.058	.062	.065	.069	.070	.069	.075	Jul
.016	.022	.026	.039	.042	.047	.044	.047	.051	.055	.059	.059	.059	.064	Aug
.007	.012	.016	.029	.032	.037	.035	.037	.041	.045	.049	.049	.049	.054	Sep
.000	.005	.008	.021	.025	.029	.027	.029	.033	.037	.041	.041	.041	.046	Oct
.002	.007	.011	.024	.027	.032	.029	.032	.035	.039	.043	.044	.043	.048	Nov
.002	.008	.012	.025	.028	.032	.030	.032	.036	.040	.044	.045	.044	.049	Dec
	.005	.009	.022	.025	.030	.028	.030	.034	.038	.041	.042	.041	.047	**1991** Jan
		.004	.017	.020	.024	.022	.024	.028	.032	.036	.037	.036	.041	Feb
			.013	.016	.021	.018	.021	.024	.028	.032	.033	.032	.037	Mar
				.003	.008	.005	.008	.011	.015	.019	.020	.019	.024	Apr
					.004	.002	.004	.008	.012	.016	.016	.016	.021	May
						.000	.000	.004	.007	.011	.012	.011	.016	Jun
							.002	.006	.010	.013	.014	.013	.019	Jul
								.004	.007	.011	.012	.011	.016	Aug
									.004	.007	.008	.007	.013	Sep
										.004	.004	.004	.009	Oct
											.001	.000	.005	Nov
												.000	.004	Dec
													.005	**1992** Jan

Corporation Tax

Rates

Financial years†	1987	1988	1989	1990	1991	1992
Rate (%)	35	35	35	34	33	33
ACT fraction	$27/73$	$1/3$	$1/3$	$1/3$	$1/3$	$1/3$
Small companies rate *						
(profits below £100,000)	27	25				
(profits below £150,000)			25			
(profits below £200,000)				25		
(profits below £250,000)					25	25
Small companies fraction *						
(profits £100,000 - £500,000)	$1/50$	$1/40$				
(profits £150,000 - £750,000)			$1/40$			
(profits £200,000 - £1,000,000)				$1/40$		
(profits £250,000 - £1,250,000)					$1/40$	$1/40$

* Does not apply to a close investment-holding company (s 13A TA 1988).
† The financial year 1992 starts on 1.4.92 and ends on 31.3.92 (and similarly
for references embodying other dates).

Small companies marginal relief

Lower and upper relevant amounts are reduced for short accounting periods and associated companies.
The small companies fraction is applied to:

$$(M - P) \times \frac{I}{P} \quad \text{to provide the relief from tax at full rate on I.}$$

M = Upper Relevant Maximum Amount (ie £1,250,000 in 1991 and 1992)
P = Profits (being the profits on which tax falls finally to be borne and franked investment income but excludes group income)
I = Basic Profits (being the profits on which tax falls finally to be borne)
(before 16.3.87 I = income).

Close company abatements

Close company apportionments are abolished for accounting periods starting after 31.3.1989.

Trading company estate income abatement:
  Calculate $\quad \dfrac{\text{estate income}}{\text{estate + trading income}} = A$
  (a) If estate income is less than £75,000 x A ("the upper limit") then it can be reduced by one half of the amount by which the upper limit exceeds the estate income; or
  (b) If estate income is less than £25,000 x A it can be ignored.

Investment income abatement:
Deduction of lesser of:
  (a) 10% of estate or trading income; and
  (b) £1,000 (or £3,000 if a trading company or member of a trading group).

Income tax rates

Taxable income £	Band £	Rate %	Tax on band - £	Cumulative tax - £
1992/93				
Up to 2,000	2,000	20	400	400
2,001 – 23,700	21,700	25	5,425	5,825
Over 23,700		40		
1991/92				
Up to 23,700	23,700	25	5,925	5,925
Over 23,700		40		
1990/91				
Up to 20,700	20,700	25	5,175	5,175
Over 20,700		40		
1989/90				
Up to 20,700	20,700	25	5,175	5,175
Over 20,700		40		
1988/89				
Up to 19,300	19,300	25	4,825	4,825
Over 19,300		40		
1987/88				
Up to 17,900	17,900	27	4,833	4,833
17,901 - 20,400	2,500	40	1,000	5,833
20,401 - 25,400	5,000	45	2,250	8,083
25,401 - 33,300	7,900	50	3,950	12,033
33,301 -41,200	7,900	55	4,345	16,378
Over 41,200		60		

Additional rate on trusts

Additional rate of tax charged on discretionary and accumulation trusts:

1992/93	10%
1991/92	10%
1990/91	10%
1989/90	10%
1988/89	10%
1987/88	18%

Income Tax Reliefs

	1987/88	1988/89	1989/90	1990/91	1991/92	1992/93
Personal allowance*:	-	-	-	3,005	3,295	3,445
Married couple's allowance*:	-	-	-	1,720	1,720	1,720
Former personal allowances:						
• Married*	3,795	4,095	4,375	-	-	-
• Single	2,425	2,605	2,785	-	-	-
Wife's earned income allowance	2,425	2,605	2,785	-	-	-
Age allowances:						
Personal allowance (over 75)*	-	-	-	3,820	4,180	4,370
Personal allowance (under 75)*	-	-	-	3,670	4,020	4,200
Married couple's allowance (over 75)*	-	-	-	2,185	2,395	2,505
Married couple's allowance (under 75)*	-	-	-	2,145	2,355	2,465
• Married (over 75†)	4,845	5,205	5,565	-	-	-
• Married (under 75†)	4,675	5,035	5,385	-	-	-
• Single (over 75†)	3,070	3,310	3,540	-	-	-
• Single (under 75†)	2,960	3,180	3,400	-	-	-
Income limit*	9,800	10,600	11,400	12,300	13,500	14,200
Not beneficial if income exceeds:						
Married (over 75†)	11,375	12,265	13,780	14,860	16,620	17,620
Married (under 75†)	11,120	12,010	13,420	14,480	16,220	17,200
Single (over 75†)	10,767.50	11,657.50	12,910	13,930	15,270	16,050
Single (under 75†)	10,602.50	11,462.50	12,630	13,630	14,950	15,710
Additional personal allowance	1,370	1,490	1,590	1,720	1,720	1,720
Blind person's allowance	540	540	540	1,080	1,080	1,080
Daughter's or son's services	55	-	-	-	-	-
Dependent relative relief *:						
• women claimants (unless married)	145	-	-	-	-	-
• other claimants	100	-	-	-	-	-
Housekeeper relief	100	-	-	-	-	-
Widow's bereavement allowance	1,370	1,490	1,590	1,720	1,720	1,720

See next page   † *Before 1989/90, the age limit was 80*

The following is a checklist of some income tax reliefs and other provisions:

- *Additional Personal Allowance* - available mainly to a person with whom a "qualifying child" lives, when the married person's relief cannot be claimed. From 6.4.89 only one allowance for an unmarried couple living together with children.
- *Age Allowances* - where the income limit is exceeded the deduction is reduced by two thirds of the excess until the normal personal relief is reached. From 1989/90 the reduction is one half of the excess.
- *Beneficial Loans* - see page 25. No charge if "cash equivalent" does not exceed £300 in YA (from 1991/92).
- *Business Expansion Scheme* - maximum investment of £40,000 in YA available as a deduction against total income. Minimum investment of £500 in any one company in YA to qualify for relief (unless through "approved fund"). From 6.4.87, relief on shares issued before 6 Oct in YA may be claimed partly in preceding YA.
  BES income tax relief available for issues up to 31.12.93.
- *Capital Allowances* - see page 34.
- *Covenants* - see page 25.
- *Daughter's or son's services* - this relief is abolished for 1988/89 onwards.
- *Enterprise Zones* – 100% Initial Allowance available for expenditure (no limit on amount of expenditure) on Enterprise Zone Property; see Capital Allowances.
- *Flat Rate Allowances* for upkeep of tools and special clothing - see pages 31 and 32.
- *Gift aid* - from 1.10.90, tax relief on single charitable gifts which equal or exceed £400 (£600 from 1.10.90 to 30.6.92) (net of basic rate income tax) without a maximum limit (before 19.3.91 up to £5m limit per donor per tax year).
- *Interest received* from banks, building societies etc. – Anyone who does not have to pay income tax can fill in a simple form to stop tax being deducted from interest received after 5.4.91 (see tax guides IR 110 – 112).
- *Interest received* on damages for personal injuries or death - is exempt.
- *Life assurance* - relief available for pre-14.3.84 policies - 12.5% for 1988/89 onwards (previously 15%).
- *Maintenance Payments* – Since 15.3.88 only certain payments qualify for relief. Relief cannot be greater than the married couple's Allowance and ceases if recipient remarries.
- *Married Couple's Allowance* - in year of marriage is reduced by one twelfth for each complete tax month before marriage. This allowance will go to the husband but if he has insufficient income any surplus can be transferred to his wife.

From 1993/94 married couples can choose how to allocate the allowance between them (a wife has the right to claim half the allowance).

- *Married Man's Allowance* - in year of marriage is reduced by one twelfth of excess over single allowance for each complete tax month before marriage. This allowance abolished from 6.4.90.
- *Mortgage Interest Paid* - relief (from 6.4.91 restricted to relief at basic rate) against total income for interest on first £30,000 borrowed per residence for purchase or (if loan or written offer made before 6.4.88) improvement of land or buildings used as the only or main residence of the borrower or certain others (not dependent relatives for most loans made from 6.4.88).
- *National Insurance Contributions* (Class 4) - relief against total income for one half of the contributions for 1985/86 onwards.
- *National Savings* - exemption for first £70 interest on ordinary accounts (husband and wife can each have exemption). Exemption for interest and bonus on Children's Bonus Bond.
- *Non-taxable State benefits* - see page 58.
- *Payroll deduction scheme* - tax relief on charitable donations through approved scheme. Maximum donations of £600 from 1990/91 (£480 in 1989/90; £240 in 1988/89; £120 in 1987/88).
- *Personal Allowance* - available to every individual taxpayer to set against all types of income.
- *PEPs* - maximum investment of £6,000 from 1990/91 (previously £4,800 in 1989/90; £3,000 in 1988 and £2,400 in 1987); dividends and reinvested interest are tax free. Also, from 1.1.92 a maximum investment of £3,000 per tax year in a single-company PEP.
- *Personal Pension Schemes* – see page 26.
- *Private medical insurance* - relief on premiums for eligible insurance for those aged 60 or over from 6.4.90.
- *Profit-Related Pay* (PRP) - one half (from 1.4.91, all) of PRP is exempt up to a limit which is the lower of 20% of PAYE pay or £4,000 p.a. (£3,000 p.a. before 1.4.89).
- *Repayment Supplements* - (see page 39) are exempt.
- *Retirement Annuities* - see pages 26 and 27.
- *Share and Share Option Schemes* - there are tax reliefs under approved schemes.
- *Small maintenance payments* - see page 25 (for pre-15.3.88 orders).
- *Tax Exempt Special Savings Account* (TESSA) - from 1.1.91, maximum savings of £9,000 over 5 years; interest is tax free provided capital undisturbed for 5 years.
- *Termination payments* - exemption for the first £30,000 (before 6.4.88 - £25,000, with reductions of 50% and 25% on the tax charged on the next two £25,000 slices).
- *Vocational training* – from 6.4.92 tax relief for payment by trainee for own vocational training.

Wife's earnings election

The wife's earnings election arrangements do not apply to tax years 1990/91 onwards. Prior to the introduction of independent taxation a married couple may have found it to their advantage to elect for the separate taxation of the wife's earnings. This would normally only be worthwhile if the couple's combined income before deduction of allowances and reliefs reaches a certain amount (which includes a further minimum amount of wife's earned income):-

	Minimum joint income	Minimum wife's earned income
1987/88	£26,870	£6,545
1988/89	£28,484	£6,579
1989/90	£30,511	£7,026

Fixed profit car scheme

This is an administrative arrangement (revised for 1990/91 onwards) which may be used to simplify the collection of any income tax due on motor mileage allowances paid by employers to employees. The "tax-free" rates per mile are intended to reflect the tax-allowable costs of using a private car for business purposes:

	Cylinder capacity – cc	Business use (miles p.a.) 0 -4,000	4,000 and over
1990/91	0 to 1,000	24.5p	9.5p
	1,001 to 1,500	30.0p }32p*	11.5p }12.5p*
	1,501 to 2,000	34.0p	13.5p
	2,000 +	43.0p	16.5p
1991/92	0 to 1,000	24.5p	11.0p
	1,001 to 1,500	30.0p }32p*	13.0p }14.5p*
	1,501 to 2,000	34.0p	16.0p
	2,000 +	45.0p	20.5p
1992/93	0 to 1,000	25.0p	14.0p
	1,001 to 1,500	30.0p }34p*	17.0p }19.0p*
	1,501 to 2,000	38.0p	21.0p
	2,000 +	51.0p	27.0p

* Where employers pay the same rate whatever the cylinder capacity the average of the two middle bands applies (ie in 1990/91 32p for the first 4,000 miles and 12.5p thereafter).

Car fuel benefit

	Cylinder capacity cc OR	Original market value of cars with no cylinder capacity	Business use (miles p.a.) 0 - 17,999		18,000 +	
			Petrol	Diesel	Petrol	Diesel
1987/88 -	0 to 1,400	0 to 5,999 *	£480	£480	£240	£240
1991/92	1,400 + to 2,000	6,000 to 8,499	£600	£600	£300	£300
	2,000 +	8,500 +	£900	£900	£450	£450
1992/93	0 to 1,400	0 to 5,999 *	£500	£460	£250	£230
	1,400 + to 2,000	6,000 to 8,499	£630	£460	£315	£230
	2,000 +	8,500 +	£940	£590	£470	£295

For VAT on fuel for private use, see page 71.   * ie under £6,000

Car Benefit

> It is intended to introduce scale charges based wholly on price as soon as practicable

Tax year	Original market value £	Cylinder capacity cc	Original market value of cars without cylinder capacity £	Age at end of year of assessment: Under 4 years Business use (miles p.a.) 0-2,500	2,501-17,999	18,000+	4 years or more Business use (miles p.a.) 0-2,500	2,501-17,999	18,000+
87/88	up to 19,250	0 - 1,400	0 - 5,999	787.50	525.00	262.50	525.00	350.00	175.00
		1,400+ to 2,000	6,000-8,499	1,050.00	700.00	350.00	705.00	470.00	235.00
		2,000 +	8,500-19,250	1,650.00	1,100.00	550.00	1,087.50	725.00	362.50
	19,250+		19,250+	2,175.00	1,450.00	725.00	1,455.00	970.00	485.00
	29,000+		29,000 +	3,450.00	2,300.00	1,150.00	2,295.00	1,530.00	765.00
88/89	up to 19,250	0 - 1,400	0 - 5,999	1,575.00	1,050.00	525.00	1,050.00	700.00	350.00
		1,400+ to 2,000	6,000-8,499	2,100.00	1,400.00	700.00	1,410.00	940.00	470.00
		2,000 +	8,500-19,250	3,300.00	2,200.00	1,100.00	2,175.00	1,450.00	725.00
	19,250 +		19,250 +	4,350.00	2,900.00	1,450.00	2,910.00	1,940.00	970.00
	29,000+		29,000 +	6,900.00	4,600.00	2,300.00	4,590.00	3,060.00	1,530.00
89/90	up to 19,250	0 - 1,400	0 - 5,999	2,100.00	1,400.00	700.00	1,425.00	950.00	475.00
		1,400+ to 2,000	6,000-8,499	2,775.00	1,850.00	925.00	1,875.00	1,250.00	625.00
		2,000+	8,500-19,250	4,425.00	2,950.00	1,475.00	2,925.00	1,950.00	975.00
	19,250+			5,775.00	3,850.00	1,925.00	3,900.00	2,600.00	1,300.00
	29,000+			9,225.00	6,150.00	3,075.00	6,150.00	4,100.00	2,050.00
90/91	up to 19,250	0 - 1,400	0 - 5,999	2,550.00	1,700.00	850.00	1,725.00	1,150.00	575.00
		1,400+ to 2,000	6,000-8,499	3,300.00	2,200.00	1,100.00	2,250.00	1,500.00	750.00
		2,000+	8,500-19,250	5,325.00	3,550.00	1,775.00	3,525.00	2,350.00	1,175.00
	19,250+			6,900.00	4,600.00	2,300.00	4,650.00	3,100.00	1,550.00
	29,000+			11,100.00	7,400.00	3,700.00	7,350.00	4,900.00	2,450.00
91/92	up to 19,250	0 - 1,400	0 - 5,999	3,075.00	2,050.00	1,025.00	2,100.00	1,400.00	700.00
		1,400+ to 2,000	6,000-8,499	3,975.00	2,650.00	1,325.00	2,700.00	1,800.00	900.00
		2,000+	8,500-19,250	6,375.00	4,250.00	2,125.00	4,275.00	2,850.00	1,425.00
	19,250+			8,250.00	5,500.00	2,750.00	5,550.00	3,700.00	1,850.00
	29,000+			13,350.00	8,900.00	4,450.00	8,850.00	5,900.00	2,950.00
92/93	up to 19,250	0 - 1,400	0 - 5,999	3,210.00	2,140.00	1,070.00	2,190.00	1,460.00	730.00
		1,400+ to 2,000	6,000-8,499	4,155.00	2,770.00	1,385.00	2,820.00	1,880.00	940.00
		2,000+	8,500-19,250	6,660.00	4,440.00	2,220.00	4,470.00	2,980.00	1,490.00
	19,250+			8,625.00	5,750.00	2,875.00	5,805.00	3,870.00	1,935.00
	29,000+			13,950.00	9,300.00	4,650.00	9,255.00	6,170.00	3,085.00

Mobile Telephone Benefit

From 6.4.91, an employee receiving the benefit of private use of a mobile (including car) telephone will pay tax on a standard amount of £200 p.a. for each telephone.

Automobile Association Schedule
of estimated standing and running costs
(petrol cars) (April 1991)

	Engine capacity (cc): Up to 1,000	1,001 to 1,400	1,401 to 2,000	2,001 to 3,000	3,001 to 4,500
Standing charges per annum (£)					
(a) Car licence	100.00	100.00	100.00	100.00	100.00
(b) Insurance	499.71	615.98	725.52	1,185.00	1,325.76
(c) Depreciation (based on 10,000 miles p.a.)	866.85	1,223.42	1,624.06	3,061.25	3,949.87
(d) Subscription	56.25	56.25	56.25	56.25	56.25
	1,522.81	1,995.65	2,505.83	4,402.50	5,431.88
Cost per mile (in pence)					
5,000 miles	30.456	39.913	50.117	88.050	108.638
10,000 miles	15.228	19.956	25.058	44.025	54.318
15,000 miles	11.308	14.935	18.871	33.432	41.479
20,000 miles	10.215	13.648	17.401	31.196	39.009
25,000 miles	9.558	12.876	16.519	29.855	37.527
30,000 miles	7.965	10.730	13.766	24.879	31.272
Running cost per mile (in pence)					
(e) Petrol *	5.227 (5.712)	5.974 (6.528)	6.970 (7.616)	9.504 (10.386)	10.455 (11.425)
(f) Oil	0.527	0.527	0.561	0.618	1.011
(g) Tyres	0.528	0.689	0.834	1.605	2.068
(h) Servicing	1.089	1.089	1.089	1.420	2.121
(i) Repairs and replacements	4.995	5.288	6.180	9.351	11.622
pence	12.366 (12.851)	13.567 (14.121)	15.634 (16.280)	22.498 (23.380)	27.277 (28.247)

* Unleaded petrol at £2.09 per gallon - 46.03p. per litre.
Figures in brackets for leaded petrol at £2.28 per gallon - 50.2p. per litre.
For every penny more or less, add or subtract: 0.025   0.028   0.033   0.045   0.050

Total of standing and running costs (in pence) based on annual mileages of:

	Engine capacity (cc): Up to 1,000	1,001 to 1,400	1,401 to 2,000	2,001 to 3,000	3,001 to 4,500
Unleaded petrol					
5,000 miles	42.822	53.480	65.751	110.548	135.915
10,000 miles	27.594	33.523	40.692	66.523	81.595
15,000 miles	23.674	28.502	34.505	55.930	68.756
20,000 miles	22.581	27.215	33.035	53.694	66.286
25,000 miles	21.924	26.443	32.153	52.353	64.804
30,000 miles	20.331	24.297	29.400	47.377	58.549
Leaded petrol					
5,000 miles	43.307	54.034	66.397	111.430	136.885
10,000 miles	28.079	34.077	41.338	67.405	82.565
15,000 miles	24.159	29.056	35.151	56.812	69.726
20,000 miles	23.066	27.769	33.681	54.576	67.256
25,000 miles	22.409	26.997	32.799	53.235	65.774
30,000 miles	20.816	24.851	30.046	48.259	59.519

(Reproduced with the kind permission of the Automobile Association which produces a separate schedule in respect of diesel cars.)

Notes

a.   *Road tax.*

b.   *Insurance* - this is the average cost for a fully comprehensive policy. No allowance is made for a no-claims discount.

c.   *Depreciation* - this is based on the average cost of a new car and assuming an economical life of 80,000 miles or eight years. The figure is therefore adjusted to take into account the car's annual mileage, but in the case of second hand cars the depreciation should be assessed individually.

d.   *AA Membership* subscription including Relay.

e.   *Fuel* - the average price of a gallon of petrol or diesel is given on the individual leaflets and the cost per mile figure is calculated from what we consider to be a reasonable fuel consumption for the various engine capacity groups.

f.   *Engine Oil* - allowance is made for normal oil consumption and routine oil changes.

g.   *Tyres* - estimated tyre life of 30,000 miles.

h.   *Servicing* - routine servicing as recommended by the vehicle manufacturers. In the case of older motor cars servicing costs may be more.

i.   *Repairs and Replacements* - estimated on the basis of the total cost of repairs, replacements and renovations over 8 years or 80,000 miles.

Interest on beneficial loans

A charge to income tax may arise on the cash equivalent of a beneficial loan. The cash equivalent is the difference between the amount of interest at the official rate and the amount of any interest actually paid. No charge arises if the cash equivalent does not exceed £300 from YA 1991/92 (£200 in YA 1980/81 to 1990/91). No charge arises if the person employed is neither an employee earning £8,500 p.a. or more nor a director.

Period	Official Rate % p.a.	Period	Official Rate % p.a.	Period	Official Rate % p.a.
6.5.80 - 5.10.82	15.0	6.8.88 - 5.10.88	12.0	6.4.91 - 5.5.91	13.5
6.10.82 - 5.4.87	12.0	6.10.88 - 5.1.89	13.5	6.5.91 - 5.7.91	12.75
6.4.87 - 5.6.87	11.5	6.1.89 - 5.7.89	14.5	6.7.91 - 5.8.91	12.25
6.6.87 - 5.9.87	10.5	6.7.89 - 5.11.89	15.5	6.8.91 - 5.10.91	11.75
6.9.87 - 5.12.87	11.5	6.11.89 - 5.11.90	16.5	6.10.91 - 5.3.92	11.25
6.12.87 - 5.5.88	10.5	6.11.90 - 5.3.91	15.5	6.3.92 - 5.6.92	10.75
6.5.88 - 5.8.88	9.5	6.3.91 - 5.4.91	14.5	6.6.92 - 5.11.92	10.5
				6.11.92 -	9.75

Covenanted payments

Covenantor	Covenantee	Period covenant must be capable of exceeding (years)	Notes
Individual	Charity	3	Normally no limit from 1986/7. No higher rate relief for an amount in YA exceeding £3,000 (1981/82 & 1982/83); £5,000 (1983/84 & 1984/85); or £10,000 (1985/86).
	Any person (other than spouse or unmarried child under 18)*	6	No tax effect if covenant made on or after 15.3.88 or made before but not received by IR by 30.6.88. In any event no higher rate relief.†
Company	Charity	3	

* There are special provisions for payments to former spouses, business partners etc and new rules apply for maintenance arrangements made from 15.3.88.
† If received after 30.6.88 may be effective for any payments due before 15.3.88.

Small maintenance payments

Payments under small maintenance orders are made without deduction of income tax. The payer can claim a deduction in computing total income. The payee is chargeable under Schedule D III. These provisions only apply to payments under court orders made pre-15.3.88 and certain other orders.

Payments due	Payments not to exceed: Weekly: To spouse or former spouse for their benefit	To any person under 21 years for their benefit	To any person for the benefit of a person under 21 yrs	Monthly: To spouse or former spouse for their benefit	To any person under 21 years for their benefit	To any person for the benefit of a person under 21 yrs
	(a)	(b)	(c)	(a)	(b)	(c)
6.4.86 onwards	£48	£48	£25	£208	£208	£108

Personal pension schemes

Inland Revenue agreed early retirement ages

Personal pension schemes can provide for the annuity to commence before the age of 50 if the member's occupation is one in which persons customarily retire before that age. The following are agreed early retirement ages:

Occupation	Age	Occupation	Age	Occupation	Age
Athletes	35	Golfers	40	Rugby League players	35
Badminton players	35	Jockeys (flat racing)	45	Skiers (downhill)	30
Boxers	35	Jockeys (National Hunt)	35	Speedway riders	40
Cricketers	40	Models	35	Squash players	35
Cyclists	35	Motor Cycle riders (Moto-		Table tennis players	35
Dancers	35	cross or Road Racing)	40	Tennis players (inc. Real	
Divers (saturation, deep		Motor racing drivers	40	Tennis)	35
sea & free swimming)	40	Royal Marine reservists		Trapeze artists	40
Footballers	35	(non-commissioned)	45	Wrestlers	35

The ages shown above for professional sports players apply only to arrangements made in respect of relevant earnings (eg tournament earnings, appearance and prize money) from activities as professional players. They do not apply to relevant earnings from sponsorship or coaching for which, if desired, a separate arrangement with a pension age within the normal range should be made.

Members' contributions

Normal limit: 17.5% of net relevant earnings for year of assessment ("NRE") (or higher if over 50 (or, from 1989/90, over 35) at beginning of year of assessment - see Tables below).
Lump sum on death of member: 5% of NRE (included within the above limit).
Relief is reduced if there are also qualifying premiums under retirement annuity contracts.

Tax year 1988/89		*Tax years 1989/90 onwards*	
Age	Limit (%)	Age	Limit(%)
51 - 55	20	36 - 45	20
56 - 60	22.5	46 - 50	25
61 or more	27.5	51 - 55	30
		56 - 60	35
		61 or more	40

For 1989/90 onwards there is a limit (the "earnings cap") on the amount of earnings from which contributions will receive tax relief:

1989/90	£60,000
1990/91	£64,800
1991/92	£71,400
1992/93	£75,000

The cap applies to all personal pension schemes (and occupational pension schemes set up since 14.3.89 and people joining any occupational scheme from 1.6.89).

Retirement annuities

These provisions apply to schemes where contributions were first paid before 1 July 1988.

Inland Revenue agreed early retirement ages

Occupation	Age	Occupation	Age	Occupation	Age
Air pilots	55	Martial arts instructors	50	Physiotherapists (female)	55
Brass instrumentalists	55	Midwives (female)	55	Psychiatrists (maximum	
Circus animal trainers	50	Moneybroker dealers	50	part-time NHS specialists)	55
Croupiers	50	Moneybroker managers		Royal Navy reservists	50
Firemen (part-time)	55	& directors	55	Rugby League referees	50
Fishermen (inshore or		Newscasters (ITV)	50	Singers	55
distant water)	55	Nurses (female)	55	Territorial Army members	50
Health visitors (female)	55	Off-shore riggers	50		
Interdealer brokers	50				

Qualifying premiums

Normal limit: 17.5% of NRE (or higher, if born in or before 1933 (for tax years 1982/83 to 1986/87) or over 50 at beginning of year of assessment (1987/88 onwards) - see Tables below).
Contracts for dependants/lump sum: 5% of NRE (included within the above limit).

Tax years 1982/83 to 1986/87		*Tax years 1987/88 onwards*	
Year of birth	*Limit (%)*	*Age*	*Limit (%)*
1916 - 1933	20	51 - 55	20
1914 or 1915	21	56 - 60	22.5
1912 or 1913	24	61 or more	27.5
1910 or 1911	26.5		
1908 or 1909	29.5		
1907 or earlier	32.5		

Partnership retirement annuities

These are treated as earned income except to the extent they exceed:

50% * of the average of: { a former partner's (dynamised)† profit shares in the best 3 out of the last 7 years of assessment (in which he devoted substantially the whole of his time as a partner).

* From 1980/81, where the December RPI (see page 46) preceding a year of assessment is higher than in December in the retirement year of assessment (taken as 1974/75, if retired before then) the limit is increased by the percentage RPI increase.
† From 1982/83, where the December RPI in the last of the 7 years is higher than in December for any of the previous 6 years, the relevant profit shares are increased by the appropriate percentage RPI increases.

Schedule D, Cases IV and V

Liability to tax on income from securities or possessions outside the UK:

Domicile	UK residence status†	Securities	Possessions
UK	R &/or OR	Case IV	Case V *
	R & NOR	Case IV (or, if a British subject, no liability if unremitted)	Case V* (or, if a British subject, no liability if unremitted)
	NR	No liability	No liability
Non-UK	R &/or OR R & NOR	Case IV (or no liability if unremitted)	Case V (or no liability if unremitted)
	NR	No liability	No liability

* A 10% deduction is made for charging pension income.
Annuities and pensions under certain compensation schemes for victims of National Socialist persecution are exempt (50% exemption before 6.4.86 for pensions).   † R = resident; OR = ordinarily resident; NR = not resident; NOR = not ordinarily resident.

Schedule E

Liability to income tax on emoluments under Schedule E Cases I, II and III

Foreign emoluments
(Those received from non-UK resident employers by non-UK domiciliaries)

UK residence status (see above for abbreviations)	Duties performed - wholly in UK	partly in UK	partly abroad	wholly abroad
R & OR	Case I (FED)	Case I (FED)	Case I (FED)	Case III (or no liability if unremitted)
R & NOR	Case II (FED)	Case II (FED)	Case III (or no liability if unremitted)	Case III (or no liability if unremitted)
NR	Case II (FED)	Case II (FED)	No liability	No liability

Note: "FED" refers to the possible availability of the Foreign Emoluments Deduction until 1988/89. This will only be available if the person was in a foreign employment at any time from 6.4.83 to 13.3.84 (or started such employment before 1.8.84 in fulfilment of a pre-14.3.84 obligation) and has held a foreign employment in 1984/85 and each subsequent tax year (see Table in 1990/91 and previous editions of this book).

Other emoluments

UK residence status	Duties performed - wholly in UK	partly in UK	partly abroad	wholly abroad
R & OR	Case I	Case I (unless 100% * deduction) **	Case I (unless 100%* deduction) **	Case I (unless 100%* deduction)**
R & NOR	Case II	Case II	Case III (or no liability if unremitted)	Case III (or no liability if unremitted)
NR	Case II	Case II	No liability	No liability

Notes: "100% deduction" refers to the deduction available where there is a qualifying period of at least 365 days absence from the UK (which can include days in the UK if the 62 days and one sixth rules are met). There are special provisions for seafarers from 6.4.88, with new limits from 6.4.91. Also, where UK visits extended because of exceptional circumstances see SP 2/91.

* Up to 5.4.85 a deduction (12.5% in 1984/85, otherwise 25%) was available where there were at least 30 qualifying days absence from the UK.
** Up to 5.4.85 a deduction (12.5% in 1984/85, otherwise 25%) was available where there was a non-UK employer, with no minimum period of absence.

Inland Revenue Tax Guides

These guides should be available free from any office of HM Inspector of Taxes and other Tax Enquiry Centres (typical hours 10 am to 4 pm) *unless otherwise stated.*

IR 1	Extra-statutory concessions (as at 10 January 1992)
IR 6	Double taxation relief (1984)
IR 9	The tax treatment of livestock: the herd basis (1984 and 1991 insert)
IR 12	Occupational pension schemes; practice notes (1991) (£10) (also on computer disk) *(Superannuation Funds Office - see page 4)*
IR14/15	Construction industry tax deduction scheme (1982, 1989 & 1992 supplements)
IR 20	Residents' and non-residents' liability to tax in the UK (1986)
IR 24	Class 4 National Insurance contributions (1991)
IR 26	IT assessments on business profits: changes of accounting date (1982)
IR 28	Starting in business (1990)
IR 33	Income tax and school leavers (1991)
IR 34	Income tax: PAYE (1990)
IR 37	Income tax and capital gains tax: appeals (1990)
IR 40	Conditions for getting a sub-contractor's tax certificate (1991)
IR 41	Income tax and the unemployed (1991)
IR 42	Income tax: lay-offs and short-time work (1989)
IR 43	Income tax and strikes (1989)
IR 45	IT, CGT and IHT: What happens when someone dies? (1991)
IR 46	Clubs, societies and associations (1991)
IR 51	The Business Expansion Scheme (1989)
IR 52	Your tax office: why it is where it is (1989)
IR 53	Thinking of taking someone on? (1991)
IR 56/NI39	Employed or self-employed? (1989)
IR 57	Thinking of working for yourself? (1991)
IR 60	Income tax and students (1990)
IR 63	MIRAS: Mortgage interest relief at source (1991)
IR 64	Giving to charity: how businesses can get tax relief (1992)
IR 65	Giving to charity: how individuals can get tax relief (1991)
IR 66	Stamp duty reserve tax (1986)
IR 68	Accrued income scheme (1990)
IR 69	Expenses: forms P11D (1987)
IR 70	Computerised payroll (1987)
IR 71	PAYE: Inspection of employers' and contractors' records (1990)
IR 72	Inland Revenue investigations: the examination of business accounts (1990)
IR 73	Inland Revenue investigations: how settlements are negotiated (1989)

IR 75	Tax reliefs for charities (1987)
IR 76	Personal pension schemes: guidance notes (1991) *(Superannuation Funds Office - see page 4)*
IR 78	Personal pensions (1989)
IR 80	Independent taxation: a guide for married couples (1991)
IR 81	Independent taxation: a guide for pensioners (1990)
IR 82	Independent taxation: a guide for husbands on a low income (1990)
IR 83	Independent taxation: a guide for tax practitioners (1990)*(telephone (071) 438 7033)*
IR 84	Have you anything to declare (1989)
IR 85	Business expansion scheme: private rented housing (1989)
IR 86	Independent taxation: a guide to mortgage interest relief for married couples (1990)
IR 87	Rooms to let (1991)
IR 89	PEPs (1990)
IR 90	Independent taxation: a guide to tax allowances and reliefs (1989)
IR 91	Independent taxation: a guide for widows and widowers (1989)
IR 92	Independent taxation: a guide for one-parent families (1989)
IR 93	Separation, divorce and maintenance payments (1990)
IR 95	Shares for employees: profit-sharing schemes (1991)
IR 96	Profit-sharing schemes: explanatory notes (1990) *(Public Enquiry Room - see page 4)*
IR 97	Shares for employees: SAYE share options (1991)
IR 98	SAYE share option schemes: explanatory notes (1990) *(Public Enquiry Room - see page 4)*
IR 99	Shares for employees: executive share options (1991)
IR 100	Executive share option schemes: explanatory notes (1991) *(Public Enquiry Room - see page 4)*
IR 103	Tax relief for private medical insurance (1990)
IR 104	Simple tax accounts (1990)
IR 105	How your profits are taxed (1990)
IR 106	Capital allowances for vehicles and machinery (1990)
IR 109	PAYE: Inspection of employers' and contractors' records (1990)
IR 110	Can you stop paying tax on your bank and building society interest? (1990)

IR 111 How to claim a repayment of tax on bank and building society interest (1991)

IR 112 How to claim a repayment of income tax (1991)

IR 113 Gift aid – a guide for donors and charities (1990)

IR 114 TESSA – tax free interest for taxpayers (1990)

IR 120 You and the Inland Revenue: helping you to have your say (1991) (other versions 1992)

IR121 Income tax and pensioners (1992)

PRP2 Tax relief for Profit-Related Pay: notes for guidance (1989) *(PRP Office - see page 4)*

Stamp Duty Reserve Tax: Notes for guidance (1990) *(The Stamp Office - see page 4)]*

SO1 (SO 1 Scotland) Stamp Duty on buying a freehold house *(Stamp Offices and the Public Enquiry Room – see page 4)*

46 Q Returning payments in the entertainment industry (1983)

480 Notes on expenses payments and benefits for directors and certain employees (1991)

Miras 6 Mortgage interest and your tax relief (1982)

P 5 Farmer's guide to PAYE (1985 & 1986 & 1987 supplements)

P 7 Supplementary guide to PAYE (1991)

P 8 An employer's basic guide to PAYE (1991)

IHT 1 Inheritance tax (1991) *(Capital Taxes Office – see page 4)*

IHT 2 Inheritance tax (1990) *(Capital Taxes Office – see page 4)*

IHT 3 An introduction to inheritance tax (1989)

CA 1 Capital allowances on machinery or plant (1973 & 1989 supplement)

CA 2 Capital allowances on industrial buildings (1972 & 1989 supplement)

CA 4 Allowances for scientific research (1989)

CGT 4 Capital gains tax: owner-occupied houses (1989)

CGT 6 Retirement: disposal of a business (1989)

CGT 11 Capital gains tax and small businesses (1990)

CGT 13 Capital gains tax: the indexation allowance for quoted shares (1991)

CGT 14 Capital gains tax: an introduction (1989)

CGT 15 Capital gains tax: a guide for married couples (1990)

CGT 16 Capital gains tax: indexation allowance; disposals after 5 April 1988 (1989)

FEU 50 Payer's guide: foreign entertainers (1987) *(Foreign Entertainers Unit - see page 4)*

Business Economic Notes

BEN 1 Travel Agents (1987)

BEN 2 Road Haulage (1987)

BEN 3 The Lodging Industry (1987)

BEN 4 Hairdressers (1987)

BEN 5 Waste Materials Reclamation and Disposal (1987)

BEN 6 Funeral Directors (1987)

BEN 7 Dentists (1988)

BEN 8 Florists (1988)

BEN 9 Licensed Victuallers (1988)

BEN 10 The Jewellery Trade (1990)

BEN 11 Electrical Retailers (1990)

BEN 12 Antiques and Fine Art Dealers (1990)

BEN 13 The Pet Industry (1991) (£1)

BEN 14 Fish & Chip Shops (1991) (£1)

BEN 15 Veterinary Surgeons (1991) (£1)

BEN 16 Catering – General (1991) (£1)

BEN 17 Catering – Restaurants (1991) (£1)

BEN 16 Catering – Fast-foods (1991) (£1)

(All price 60p (unless otherwise shown), post free, from Reference Room, Inland Revenue Library (see page 4).)

Guidelines

Guidelines on the Tax Treatment of Disaster Funds (1990)

Business Expansion Scheme approved fund guidelines (1990) *(telephone (071) 438 6720)*

List 3 Fees and subscriptions paid to professional bodies (August 1991) *(£5 from Reference Room (see page 4))*

Explan- Controlled foreign companies
atory legislation (1990) *(£10 from Reference
Notes Room (see page 4))* (and see excluded countries list annexed to 8.3.91 Press Release)

A first guide to corporation tax pay and file (1991)

Tax Bulletin

The first issue of *Tax Bulletin* was published in November 1991 and is intended for "tax professionals" (to find out more, contact Inland Revenue Press Office, telephone (071) 438 6692).

Flat Rate Allowances

Extra-statutory concession A1 (as at 10 January 1992) - An employee who has to bear the cost of upkeep of tools or special clothing necessary for his work is entitled, under s 198(1) TA 1988, to a tax deduction for the expenditure incurred. For most trades flat rate expense deductions have been agreed with the trade unions concerned. These deductions are given without enquiry as to the amount of expenditure actually incurred by individual employees, provided that it is the employees' responsibility to bear the relevant cost in full. If the employer provides or pays for what is required, or would make such provision if requested, the expense cannot be regarded as necessarily incurred by the employee and no deduction is due. If the employer makes partial provision, the rate of deduction may be reduced accordingly. The existence of a flat rate allowance does not debar an individual employee from instead claiming a deduction for the actual expense he has incurred. (The terms "all workers" and "all other workers" below refer to all manual workers or others who bear the cost of upkeep of tools or special clothing and not to other employees such as office staff (from ESC A1 (1985)).)

Industry (IR Industry code)	Occupation	Deductions – £		
		87/88-88/89	89/90-90/91	91/92
Agriculture (10)	All workers	50	50	60
Aluminium (100)	(a) Continual casting operators, process operators, de-dimplers, driers, drill punchers, dross unloaders, firemen, furnace operators and their helpers, leaders, mouldmen, pourers, remelt department labourers, roll flatteners	90	95	110
	(b) cable hands, case makers, labourers, mates, truck drivers and measurers, storekeepers	45	45	50
	(c) Apprentices	30	35	40
	(d) All other workers	70	75	85
Banks (330)	Uniformed bank employees	25	30	30
Brass and Copper (90)	All workers	70	75	85
Building (270)	(a) Joiners, carpenters	80	80	90
	(b) Cement works, roofing felt and asphalt labourers	40	40	45
	(c) Labourers and navvies	25	30	30
	(d) All other workers	60	60	70
Building materials (250)	(a) Stone-masons	60	60	70
	(b) Tilemakers, labourers	25	30	30
	(c) All other workers	40	40	45
Clothing (190)	(a) Lacemakers, hosiery bleachers, dyers, scourers and knitters, knitwear bleachers and dyers	30	35	40
	(b) All other workers	20	25	25
Constructional engineering (150)	(a) Blacksmiths and their strikers, burners, caulkers,chippers, drillers, erectors, fitters, holders up, markers off, platers, riggers, riveters, rivet heaters, scaffolders, sheeters, template workers, turners, welders	80	85	95
	(b) Banksmen labourers, shop-helpers, slewers, straighteners	45	45	50
	(c) Apprentices, storekeepers	30	35	40
	(d) All other workers	55	55	65
Electrical and Electricity supply (170)	(a) Those workers incurring laundry costs only (generally CEGB employees)	15	15	20
	(b) All other workers	65	70	75
Engineering (110)	(a) Pattern makers	85	90	105
	(b) Labourers, supervisory and unskilled workers	45	45	50
	(c) Apprentices, storekeepers	30	35	40
	(d) Motor mechanics in garage repair shops	70	75	85
	(e) All other workers	70	75	85
Food (220)	All workers	25	30	30
Forestry (20)	All workers	50	50	60
Glass (240)	All workers	45	45	50
Heating (280)	(a) Pipe fitters, plumbers	75	80	90
	(b) Coverers, laggers, domestic glaziers, heating engineers and all their mates	65	70	75
	(c) All gas workers; all other workers	50	50	60
Iron & Steel (70)	(a) Day labourers, general labourers, stockmen, time keepers, warehouse staff and weighmen	45	45	50
	(b) Apprentices	30	35	40
	(c) All other workers	85	90	105
Iron Mining (50)	(a) Fillers, miners, underground workers	70	75	85
	(b) All other workers	55	55	65

Industry	Worker category			
Leather (210)	(a) Curriers (wet workers), fellmongering workers, tanning operatives (wet)	40	40	45
	(b) All other workers	25	30	30
Particular engineering (140)	(a) Pattern makers	85	90	105
	(b) All chainmakers; cleaners, galvanisers, tinners and wire drawers in the wire drawing industry; tool makers in the lock-making industry	70	75	85
	(c) Apprentices, storekeepers	30	35	40
	(d) All other workers	45	45	50
Police Force (355)	Uniformed police officers (ranks up to and including Chief Inspector)	40	40	45
Precious metals (160)	All workers	50	50	60
Printing (230)	(a) Letterpress Section: Electrical engineers (rotary presses), electrotypers, ink and roller makers, machine minders (rotary), maintenance engineers (rotary presses), stereotypers	75	80	90
	(b) Bench hands (P&B), compositors (Lp), readers (Lp), T&E Section wire room operators, warehousemen (Ppr box)	20	25	25
	(c) All other workers	50	50	60
Prisons (320)	Uniformed prison officers	40	40	45
Public service (300)	(i) Dock and inland waterways:			
	(a) Dockers, dredger drivers, hopper steerers	40	40	45
	(b) All other workers	25	30	30
	(ii) Public transport:			
	(a) Garage hands including cleaners	40	40	45
	(b) Conductors and drivers	25	30	30
Quarrying (60)	All workers	50	50	60
Railways (290)	(See the appropriate category for craftsmen, eg engineers, vehicle builders, etc) All other workers	50	50	60
Seamen (30)	(a) Carpenters (Seamen) - Passenger liners	120	125	140
	(b) Carpenters (Seamen) - Cargo vessels, tankers, coasters and ferries	90	95	110
	(c) Other Seamen - Passenger liners (1982/83 & 1983/84 only)	nil	nil	nil
	(d) Other Seamen - Cargo vessels, tankers, coasters and ferries (1982/83 & 1983/84 only)	nil	nil	nil
Shipyards (120)	(a) Blacksmiths and their strikers, boilermakers, burners, carpenters, caulkers, drillers, furnacemen (platers), holders up, fitters, platers, plumbers, riveters, sheet iron workers, shipwrights, tubers, welders	80	85	95
	(b) Labourers	45	45	50
	(c) Apprentices and storekeepers	30	35	40
	(d) All other workers	55	55	65
Textiles (180)	(a) Carders, carding engineers, overlookers (all), technicians in spinning mills	60	60	70
	(b) All other workers	45	45	50
Textile prints (200)	All workers	45	45	50
Vehicles (130)	(a) Builders, railway wagon etc repairers, railway wagon lifters	75	80	90
	(b) Railway vehicle painters and letterers, railway wagon etc builders' and repairers' assistants	45	45	50
	(c) All other workers	25	30	30
Wood and furniture (260)	(a) Carpenters, cabinet makers, joiners, wood carvers and woodcutting machinists	80	85	95
	(b) Artificial limb makers (other than in wood), organ builders, packing case makers	65	70	75
	(c) Coopers not providing own tools, labourers, polishers, upholsterers	30	35	40
	(d) All other workers	55	55	65

Uniform Allowances

The annual amounts on which income tax relief is allowed for the maintenance of officers' uniforms are given below. A reduced amount in any year may follow a change in uniform. Officers may claim additional tax relief by direct negotiation with their HM Inspector of Taxes if a larger amount than the annual allowance has been expended:

	1986/87	1987/88	1988/89	1989/90	1990/91	1991/92
Royal Navy & Royal Marines						
RN Officers of Flag rank and equivalent RM Officers	701.52	728.40	694.32	782.88	838.68	955.80
RN and RM below Flag rank	538.92	570.12	556.56	630.72	672.96	733.92
Women's Royal Navy Service Officers	335.88	340.08	298.44	331.44	337.08	373.68
Women Medical and Dental Officers RN	336.00	347.04	306.84	347.52	354.96	396.72
Queen Alexandra's Royal Navy Nursing Service						
Matrons/Chief Nursing Officers and above	512.28	394.44	437.52	465.24	472.08	513.24
Below Matron/CNO	656.40	662.76	677.40	681.96	710.52	843.48
Male QARNNS Officers (CNO and above)	348.48	352.20	332.04	387.84	413.64	445.32
Male QARNNS Officers (below CNO)	329.64	324.84	300.72	354.60	383.04	417.24
Army						
Officers serving at full mounted duty with Household Cavalry and King's Troop Royal Horse Artillery	649.06	680.22	740.58	725.34	731.43	767.35
Dismounted Officers						
Colonel and above	411.45	415.29	404.38	490.26	489.63	567.07
Below Colonel	337.47	353.35	352.85	393.28	407.93	451.66
Queen Alexandra's Royal Army Nursing Corps						
Nursing Officers Colonel and above	381.89	367.76	408.25	396.67	430.15	522.06
Non-Nursing Officers Colonel and above	350.75	338.72	372.60	381.13	388.06	441.04
Nursing Officers below Colonel	305.86	307.53	358.09	382.97	404.47	424.25
Non-Nursing Officers below Colonel	254.69	270.40	287.77	310.54	333.75	338.12
Women's Royal Army Corps, Women Officers						
Colonel and above	329.90	311.60	343.24	352.80	385.35	447.00
Below Colonel	264.94	253.88	305.63	309.23	401.29	353.00
Royal Army Medical Corps & Royal Army Dental Corps, Women Officers						
Colonel and above	336.51	344.76	379.66	369.55	382.22	478.91
Below Colonel (includes female RAMC & RADC Cadets)	309.99	321.16	377.21	389.12	427.03	363.94
Male Officers Short Service Volunteer and Limited Service Commissions	112.24	119.36	92.71	104.67	94.00	94.00
Women Officers SSVC & LSC	89.00	85.61	104.05	101.19	129.55	148.05
Royal Air Force (inc. male PMRAFNS officers)						
Air Officers	275.20	288.27	299.09	315.96	336.00	349.92
Group Captains	264.88	277.77	288.27	304.56	327.36	336.01
Wing Commander and below	245.47	257.84	268.84	287.88	312.00	306.12
Princess Mary's Royal Air Force Nursing Service						
Air Officers	272.91	282.62	287.30	319.44	346.80	408.36
Group Captains	255.72	261.92	265.82	297.00	323.28	392.04
Wing Commander and below	250.95	256.91	260.82	291.48	317.64	385.92
Women's Royal Air Force and female RAF						
Air Officers	262.49	254.91	261.04	279.84	306.60	333.84
Group Captains	246.54	246.56	252.38	270.72	297.12	327.84
Wing Commander and below	215.55	220.42	225.24	242.40	260.28	287.64

Capital Allowances

Description	Expenditure incurred after		Rate (%)
Machinery and Plant (see also "Films etc" and "Leasing". There were reduced FYAs for Teletext etc. There are special rules for ships, motor vehicles (from 11.3.92 maximum annual WDA for any business car raised to £3,000), sports grounds (inc. from 1.1.89 regulated stands) and (after 31.3.86) short-life assets. From 10.3.92 extends to capital expenditure on computer software licences	FYA WDA	21.3.1972 13.3.1984 31.3.1985 31.3.1986 26.10.1970	100 75* 50* nil* 25 (reducing balance basis)
Industrial Buildings and Structures (see also "Enterprise Zones"; "Qualifying Dwelling Houses"; "Qualifying Hotels"; "Small Workshops" and "Very Small Workshops") **	Initial WDA	12.11.1974 10.3.1981 13.3.1984 31.3.1985 31.3.1986 5.11.1962	50 75 50* 25* nil* 4 (straight line basis)
Agricultural and Forestry Land	Initial WDA	11.4.1978 31.3.1986 5.4.1946 31.3.1986	20 nil 10 4 (straight line basis)
Dredging	Initial WDA	16.1.1966 31.3.1986 5.11.1962	15 nil 4 (straight line basis)
Enterprise Zones	Initial WDA	Not more than 10 years after site first included in the zone	100 25
Films etc	FYA	9.3.1982 (expenditure treated as normal revenue expense, although, for EC films tapes or discs, capital allowances can be claimed instead†)	nil
Know-how	WDA	31.3.1986 (previously given over 6 years on a straight line basis)	25 (reducing balance basis)
Leasing	FYA	31.5.1980 (if for a qualifying purpose)	(see Machinery & Plant)
Mines, oil wells etc	Initial WDA	16.1.1966 31.3.1986 31.3.1986 (Previously WDA was on the larger of 5% or Output of period ("A") A + Est future output of residue of expenditure)	40 (on certain construction works) nil* 10 (for certain pre-trading expenditure) or 25 (both on reducing balance basis)*
Patents	WDA	31.3.1986 (previously given over at most 17 years (or any shorter patent period) on straight line basis)	25 (reducing balance basis)
Qualifying Dwelling Houses (let on assured tenancies)	Initial WDA	9.3.1982 13.3.1984 31.3.1985 31.3.1986 9.3.1984	75 50 (limited to £40,000; 25 Gtr London £60,000) nil 4
Qualifying Hotels	Initial WDA	11.4.1978 31.3.1986 11.4.1978	20 nil * 4
Scientific research		5.11.1962	100 (not on land/bldgs after 31.3.85)
Small Workshops	Initial WDA	26.3.1980 (and before 27.3.1983) 26.3.1980 (and before 27.3.1983)	100 25
Very Small Workshops	Initial WDA	26.3.1983 (and before 27.3.1985) 26.3.1983 (and before 27.3.1985)	100 25

* Transitional provisions may have preserved old allowances until 31.1.1987. There are special transitional rules for certain expenditure qualifying for a regional development grant. (The Table does not summarise all transitional provisions.)

** From 6.4.1991 toll roads will be added to the undertakings qualifying for industrial buildings allowance.

† For EC films (only) completed after 10.3.1992 an alternative write-off is available of 33 1/3 % (flat rate per year) of production (only) expenditure (with pre-production costs after 10.3.1992 attracting relief as incurred).

Certificates of Tax Deposit
Series 6

Deposits of under £100,000: the rate is shown in *bold italic* type in the table below.
Deposits of £100,000 or over: the rate varies depending on the number of complete months the deposit is held in the relevant year.

From (incl. date)	Held for (complete months in relevant yr)	Applied to pay tax(%)	With-drawn for cash (%)
17.2.87	-	*10.00*	*5.50*
	0 - 2*	10.00	5.50
	3 - 12	10.25	5.50
* ie, under 3			
19.2.87	-	*10.00*	*5.50*
	0 - 2	9.50	5.50
	3 - 12	10.00	5.50
20.2.87	-	*9.00*	*5.50*
	0 - 2	9.00	5.50
	3 - 12	9.75	5.50
2.3.87	-	*9.00*	*5.50*
	0 - 2	9.00	5.50
	3 - 12	9.50	5.50
6.3.87	-	*8.50*	*5.50*
	0 - 2	8.50	5.50
	3 - 12	9.00	5.50
18.3.87	-	*8.00*	*5.50*
	0 - 2	8.00	5.50
	3 - 12	8.50	5.50
3.4.87	-	*8.00*	*5.50*
	0	8.00	5.50
	1 - 12	9.00	5.50
16.4.87	-	*8.00*	*5.50*
	0	8.00	5.50
	1 - 12	9.375	5.50
28.4.87	-	*8.00*	*5.50*
	0	8.00	5.50
	1 - 12	9.125	5.50
5.5.87	-	*8.00*	*5.50*
	0 - 12	8.75	5.50
12.5.87	-	*8.00*	*5.00*
	0	8.00	5.00
	1 - 12	8.50	5.00
13.5.87	-	*8.00*	*5.00*
	0	8.00	5.00
	1 - 2	8.50	5.00
	3 - 12	8.625	5.00
21.5.87	-	*8.00*	*5.00*
	0	8.00	5.00
	1 - 2	8.25	5.00
	3 - 8	8.625	5.00
	9 - 12	8.75	5.00
22.5.87	-	*8.00*	*5.00*
	0	8.00	5.00
	1 - 2	8.25	5.00
	3 - 5	8.625	5.00
	6 - 8	8.875	5.00
	9 - 12	9.00	5.00
26.5.87	-	*8.00*	*5.00*
	0	8.00	5.00
	1 - 2	8.25	5.00
	3 - 5	8.625	5.00
	6 - 12	8.875	5.00
28.5.87	-	*8.00*	*5.00*
	0	8.00	5.00
	1 - 2	8.25	5.00
	3 - 5	9.00	5.00
	6 - 8	9.125	5.00
	9 - 12	9.25	5.00
29.5.87	-	*8.00*	*5.00*

From (incl. date)	Held for (complete months in relevant yr)	Applied to pay tax(%)	With-drawn for cash (%)
	0	8.00	5.00
	1 - 2	8.25	5.00
	3 - 5	8.75	5.00
	6 - 8	8.875	5.00
	9 - 12	9.00	5.00
2.6.87	-	*8.00*	*5.00*
	0	8.00	5.00
	1 - 2	8.25	5.00
	3 - 5	8.75	5.00
	6 - 12	8.875	5.00
4.6.87	-	*8.00*	*5.00*
	0	8.00	5.00
	1 - 2	8.25	5.00
	3 - 5	8.625	5.00
	6 - 8	8.75	5.00
	9 - 12	8.875	5.00
10.6.87	-	*8.00*	*5.00*
	0	8.00	5.00
	1 - 2	8.25	5.00
	3 - 8	8.625	5.00
	9 - 12	8.75	5.00
11.6.87	-	*8.00*	*5.00*
	0	8.00	5.00
	1 - 2	8.25	5.00
	3 - 8	8.50	5.00
	9 - 12	8.625	5.00
12.6.87	-	*8.00*	*5.00*
	0	8.00	5.00
	1 - 2	8.25	5.00
	3 - 12	8.50	5.00
16.6.87	-	*8.00*	*5.00*
	0	8.00	5.00
	1 - 2	8.25	5.00
	3 - 8	8.50	5.00
	9 - 12	8.625	5.00
17.6.87	-	*8.00*	*5.00*
	0	8.00	5.00
	1 - 2	8.25	5.00
	3 - 5	8.50	5.00
	6 - 12	8.625	5.00
22.6.87	-	*8.00*	*5.00*
	0	8.00	5.00
	1 - 2	8.25	5.00
	3 - 5	8.75	5.00
	6 - 12	9.00	5.00
24.6.87	-	*8.00*	*5.00*
	0	8.00	5.00
	1 - 2	8.25	5.00
	3 - 5	9.00	5.00
	6 - 12	9.125	5.00
25.6.87	-	*8.00*	*5.00*
	0	8.00	5.00
	1 - 2	8.25	5.00
	3 - 5	8.875	5.00
	6 - 12	9.00	5.00
30.6.87	-	*8.00*	*5.00*
	0	8.00	5.00
	1 - 2	8.25	5.00
	3 - 5	9.00	5.00
	6 - 8	9.125	5.00

From (incl. date)	Held for (complete months in relevant yr)	Applied to pay tax(%)	With-drawn for cash (%)
	9 - 12	9.25	5.00
2.7.87	-	*8.00*	*5.00*
	0	8.00	5.00
	1 - 2	8.25	5.00
	3 - 8	9.00	5.00
	9 - 12	9.125	5.00
7.7.87	-	*8.00*	*5.00*
	0	8.00	5.00
	1 - 2	8.25	5.00
	3 - 12	9.125	5.00
8.7.87	-	*8.00*	*5.00*
	0	8.00	5.00
	1 - 2	8.25	5.00
	3 - 8	9.00	5.00
	9 - 12	9.125	5.00
14.7.87	-	*8.00*	*5.00*
	0	8.00	5.00
	1 - 2	8.25	5.00
	3 - 5	9.00	5.00
	6 - 12	9.125	5.00
16.7.87	-	*8.00*	*5.00*
	0	8.00	5.00
	1 - 2	8.25	5.00
	3 - 5	9.00	5.00
	6 - 8	9.125	5.00
	9 - 12	9.25	5.00
22.7.87	-	*8.00*	*5.00*
	0	8.00	5.00
	1 - 2	8.25	5.00
	3 - 5	9.125	5.00
	6 - 8	9.25	5.00
	9 - 12	9.375	5.00
23.7.87	-	*8.00*	*5.00*
	0	8.00	5.00
	1 - 2	8.25	5.00
	3 - 5	9.25	5.00
	6 - 8	9.50	5.00
	9 - 12	9.625	5.00
27.7.87	-	*8.00*	*5.00*
	0	8.00	5.00
	1 - 2	8.25	5.00
	3 - 5	9.375	5.00
	6 - 8	9.50	5.00
	9 - 12	9.625	5.00
5.8.87	-	*8.00*	*5.00*
	0	8.00	5.00
	1 - 2	8.25	5.00
	3 - 5	9.375	5.00
	6 - 8	9.625	5.00
	9 - 12	9.75	5.00
7.8.87	-	*8.00*	*5.00*
	0	8.00	5.00
	1 - 2	8.25	5.00
	3 - 8	9.75	5.00
	9 - 12	9.875	5.00
10.8.87	-	*8.00*	*5.00*
	0	8.00	5.00
	1 - 2	8.25	5.00
	3 - 5	9.875	5.00
	6 - 12	10.00	5.00

From (incl. date)	Held for (complete months in relevant yr)	Applied to pay tax(%)	Withdrawn for cash (%)
11.8.87	-	8.00	5.00
	0	8.00	5.00
	1 - 2	8.25	5.00
	3 - 12	10.00	5.00
18.8.87	-	8.00	5.00
	0	8.00	5.00
	1 - 2	8.25	5.00
	3 - 5	9.875	5.00
	6 - 8	10.00	5.00
	9 - 12	10.125	5.00
25.8.87	-	8.00	5.00
	0	8.00	5.00
	1 - 2	8.25	5.00
	3 - 5	10.00	5.00
	6 - 8	10.25	5.00
	9 -12	10.375	5.00
2.9.87	-	8.00	5.00
	0	8.00	5.00
	1 - 2	8.25	5.00
	3 - 5	10.50	5.00
	6 - 8	10.625	5.00
	9 - 12	10.75	5.00
3.9.87	-	8.00	5.00
	0	8.00	5.00
	1 - 2	8.25	5.00
	3 - 5	10.25	5.00
	6 - 8	10.375	5.00
	9 - 12	10.50	5.00
9.9.87	-	8.00	5.00
	0	8.00	5.00
	1 - 2	8.25	5.00
	3 - 5	10.00	5.00
	6 - 8	10.25	5.00
	9 - 12	10.375	5.00
14.9.87	-	8.00	5.00
	0	8.00	5.00
	1 - 2	8.25	5.00
	3 - 5	10.00	5.00
	6 - 8	10.375	5.00
	9 - 12	10.50	5.00
15.9.87	-	8.00	5.00
	0	8.00	5.00
	1 - 2	8.25	5.00
	3 - 5	10.00	5.00
	6 - 8	10.25	5.00
	9 - 12	10.375	5.00
18.9.87	-	8.00	5.00
	0	8.00	5.00
	1 - 2	8.25	5.00
	3 - 5	9.875	5.00
	6 - 8	10.25	5.00
	9 - 12	10.375	5.00
21.9.87	-	8.00	5.00
	0	8.00	5.00
	1 - 2	8.25	5.00
	3 - 5	9.875	5.00
	6 - 8	10.125	5.00
	9 - 12	10.25	5.00
29.9.87	-	8.00	5.00
	0	8.00	5.00
	1 - 2	8.25	5.00
	3 - 5	10.00	5.00
	6 - 8	10.25	5.00
	9 - 12	10.375	5.00
6.10.87	-	8.00	5.00
	0	8.00	5.00
	1 - 2	8.25	5.00
	3 - 5	10.00	5.00
	6 - 8	10.125	5.00
	9 - 12	10.25	5.00
12.10.87	-	8.00	5.00
	0	8.00	5.00
	1 - 2	8.25	5.00

From (incl. date)	Held for (complete months in relevant yr)	Applied to pay tax(%)	Withdrawn for cash (%)
	3 - 5	10.125	5.00
	6 - 8	10.25	5.00
	9 - 12	10.375	5.00
13.10.87	-	8.00	5.00
	0	8.00	5.00
	1 - 2	9.25	5.00
	3 - 5	10.125	5.00
	6 - 8	10.25	5.00
	9 - 12	10.375	5.00
14.10.87	-	8.00	5.00
	0	8.00	5.00
	1 - 2	9.25	5.00
	3 - 5	10.00	5.00.
	6 - 8	10.125	5.00
	9 - 12	10.25	5.00
23.10.87	-	8.00	5.00
	0	8.00	5.00
	1 - 2	9.25	5.00
	3 - 5	9.875	5.00
	6 - 8	10.00	5.00
	9 - 12	10.125	5.00
26.10.87	-	8.00	5.00
	0	8.00	5.00
	1 - 2	9.00	5.00
	3 - 5	9.25	5.00
	6 - 12	9.375	5.00
27.10.87	-	8.00	5.00
	0	8.00	5.00
	1 - 12	8.50	5.00
5.11.87	-	7.50	5.00
	0	7.50	5.00
	1 - 12	8.00	5.00
24.11.87	-	7.50	5.00
	0	7.50	5.00
	1 - 12	8.50	5.00
4.12.87	-	7.50	5.00
	0	7.50	5.00
	1 - 12	8.25	5.00
7.1.88	-	7.50	5.00
	0	7.50	5.00
	1 - 2	8.25	5.00
	3 - 12	8.75	5.00
25.1.88	-	7.50	5.00
	0	7.50	5.00
	1 - 2	8.25	5.00
	3 - 5	8.50	5.00
	6 - 12	8.75	5.00
26.1.88	-	7.50	5.00
	0	7.50	5.00
	1 - 2	8.25	5.00
	3 - 12	8.50	5.00
14.3.88	-	7.50	5.00
	0	7.50	5.00
	1 - 5	8.25	5.00
	6 - 12	8.50	5.00
22.3.88	-	7.00	5.00
	0	7.00	5.00
	1 - 12	8.00	5.00
11.4.88	-	6.50	5.00
	0	6.50	5.00
	1 - 12	7.50	5.00
20.4.88	-	6.50	5.00
	0	6.50	5.00
	1 - 5	7.00	5.00
	6 - 12	7.50	5.00
18.5.88	-	6.00	5.00
	0	6.00	5.00
	1 - 5	6.50	5.00
	6 - 12	7.00	5.00
7.6.88	-	6.00	5.00
	0	6.00	5.00
	1 - 6	7.00	5.00
	6 - 12	7.50	5.00

From (incl. date)	Held for (complete months in relevant yr)	Applied to pay tax(%)	Withdrawn for cash (%)
23.6.88	-	6.00	5.00
	0	6.00	5.00
	1 - 5	7.50	5.00
	6 - 12	8.00	5.00
29.6.88	-	6.50	5.00
	0	6.50	5.00
	1 - 5	8.00	5.00
	6 - 12	8.50	5.00
5.7.88	-	7.00	5.00
	0	7.00	5.00
	1 - 5	8.50	5.00
	6 - 12	9.00	5.00
20.7.88	-	7.00	5.00
	0	7.50	5.00
	1 - 5	9.00	5.00
	6 - 12	9.50	5.00
9.8.88	-	8.00	5.00
	0	8.00	5.00
	1 - 12	9.50	5.00
30.8.88	-	9.00	5.00
	0	9.00	5.00
	1 - 12	10.50	5.00
8.11.88	-	8.50	5.00
	0	8.50	5.00
	1 - 12	10.00	5.00
1.12.88	-	9.50	5.00
	0	9.50	5.00
	1 - 12	11.00	5.00
25.5.89	-	10.50	5.00
	0	10.50	5.00
	1 - 12	12.00	5.00
9.10.89	-	11.50	5.00
	0	11.50	5.00
	1 - 12	13.00	5.00
8.10.90	-	10.50	5.00
	0	10.50	5.00
	1 - 9	12.00	5.00
	9 - 12	11.50	5.00
14.2.91	-	10.00	5.00
	0	10.00	5.00
	1 - 2	12.00	5.00
	3 - 5	11.00	5.00
	6 - 12	10.50	5.00
28.2.91	-	9.50	5.00
	0	9.50	5.00
	1 - 2	11.50	5.00
	3 - 5	11.00	5.00
	6 - 8	10.50	5.00
	9 - 12	10.00	5.00
25.3.91	-	9.00	5.00
	0	9.00	5.00
	1 - 2	11.00	5.00
	3 - 5	10.50	5.00
	6 - 12	10.00	5.00
15.4.91	-	8.50	5.00
	0	8.50	5.00
	1-2	11.00	5.00
	3-5	10.50	5.00
	6-8	10.00	5.00
	9-12	9.50	5.00
28.5.91	-	8.00	5.00
	0	8.00	5.00
	1-2	10.50	5.00
	3-5	10.00	5.00
	6-12	9.50	5.00
15.7.91	-	7.50	5.00
	0	7.50	5.00
	1-2	10.00	5.00
	3-5	9.50	5.00
	6-12	9.00	5.00
5.9.91	-	7.00	5.00
	0	7.00	5.00
	1-2	9.50	5.00
	3-12	9.00	5.00

Interest Factor Tables

The interest factor tables are used in tax offices to calculate the repayment supplement (see page 39) and interest on unpaid tax in investigation settlements (see page 39). If the rate of repayment supplement changes, the factors for the period from the date of change to the last date in the table will need amending.

Repayment Supplement				Investigation Settlements		
Example:				Example:		
CT repayment of £2,000				Omitted interest (Schedule D III) for 1975/76 of		
Relevant date:	1.10.81			£500		
Interest period ends:	5.1.84			Payment expected:	1.12.85	
Factor for 5.1.84:		2.1287		Normal due date:	1.1.76	
Less factor for 1.10.81		1.9020		Factor for 1.12.85:		2.2995
Difference		0.2267		Factor for 1.1.76:		1.3320
				Difference:		0.9675
Supplement = £2,000 x 0.2267 =		£453.40		Interest = £500 x 0.9675 = £483.75		

(Where the tax is payable in two instalments (1 January and 1 July) use the factor for the mean date (1 April) in the year of assessment. Apply the difference in factors to all that tax.)

Factors as at 1st/5th* of month

	Jan	Feb	Mar	April	May	June	July	Aug	Sept	Oct	Nov	Dec
1937	0.000			0.0075			0.015					
1938	0.030			0.0375			0.045					
1939	0.060			0.0675			0.075					
1940	0.090			0.0975			0.105					
1941	0.120			0.1275			0.135					
1942	0.150			0.1575			0.165					
1943	0.180			0.1875			0.195					
1944	0.210			0.2175			0.225					
1945	0.240			0.2475			0.255					
1946	0.270			0.2775			0.285					
1947	0.300			0.3075			0.315					
1948	0.330			0.3375			0.345					
1949	0.360			0.3675			0.375					
1950	0.390			0.3975			0.405					
1951	0.420			0.4275			0.435					
1952	0.450			0.4575			0.465					
1953	0.480			0.4875			0.495					
1954	0.510			0.5175			0.525					
1955	0.540			0.5475			0.555					
1956	0.570			0.5775			0.585					
1957	0.600			0.6075			0.615					
1958	0.630			0.6375			0.645					
1959	0.660			0.6675			0.675					
1960	0.690			0.6975			0.705					
1961	0.720			0.7275			0.735					
1962	0.750			0.7575			0.765					
1963	0.780			0.7875			0.795					
1964	0.810			0.8175			0.825					
1965	0.840	0.8425	0.845	0.8475	0.850	0.8525	0.855	0.8575	0.860	0.8625	0.865	0.8675
1966	0.870	0.8725	0.875	0.8775	0.880	0.8825	0.885	0.8875	0.890	0.8925	0.895	0.8975
1967	0.900	0.9025	0.905	0.9075	0.910	0.9133	0.9167	0.920	0.9233	0.9267	0.930	0.9333
1968	0.9367	0.940	0.9433	0.9467	0.950	0.9533	0.9567	0.960	0.9633	0.9667	0.970	0.9733
1969	0.9767	0.980	0.9833	0.9867	0.990	0.9933	0.9967	1.000	1.0033	1.0067	1.010	1.0133
1970	1.0167	1.020	1.0233	1.0267	1.030	1.0333	1.0367	1.040	1.0433	1.0467	1.050	1.0533
1971	1.0567	1.060	1.0633	1.0667	1.070	1.0733	1.0767	1.080	1.0833	1.0867	1.090	1.0933
1972	1.0967	1.100	1.1033	1.1067	1.110	1.1133	1.1167	1.120	1.1233	1.1267	1.130	1.1333
1973	1.1367	1.140	1.1433	1.1467	1.150	1.1533	1.1567	1.160	1.1633	1.1667	1.170	1.1733
1974	1.1767	1.180	1.1833	1.1867	1.190	1.1933	1.197	1.2045	1.212	1.2195	1.227	1.2345
1975	1.242	1.2495	1.257	1.2645	1.272	1.2795	1.287	1.2945	1.302	1.3095	1.317	1.3245
1976	1.332	1.3395	1.347	1.3545	1.362	1.3695	1.377	1.3845	1.392	1.3995	1.407	1.4145
1977	1.422	1.4295	1.437	1.4445	1.452	1.4595	1.467	1.4745	1.482	1.4895	1.497	1.5045
1978	1.512	1.5195	1.527	1.5345	1.542	1.5495	1.557	1.5645	1.572	1.5795	1.587	1.5945
1979	1.602	1.6095	1.617	1.6245	1.632	1.6395	1.647	1.6545	1.662	1.6695	1.677	1.6845
1980	1.692	1.702	1.712	1.722	1.732	1.742	1.752	1.762	1.772	1.782	1.792	1.802
1981	1.812	1.822	1.832	1.842	1.852	1.862	1.872	1.882	1.892	1.902	1.912	1.922
1982	1.932	1.942	1.952	1.962	1.972	1.982	1.992	2.002	2.012	2.022	2.032	2.042
1983	2.0487	2.0553*	2.062	2.0687	2.0753*	2.082	2.0887	2.0953*	2.102	2.1087	2.1153*	2.122
1984	2.1287	2.1353*	2.142	2.1487	2.1553*	2.162	2.1687	2.1753*	2.182	2.1887	2.1953*	2.202

	Jan	Feb	Mar	April	May	June	July	Aug	Sept	Oct	Nov	Dec
1985	2.2087	2.2153*	2.222	2.2287	2.2353*	2.2445	2.2537	2.2628	2.2720	2.2812	2.2903	2.2995
1986	2.3087	2.3178	2.3270	2.3362	2.3453	2.3545	2.3637	2.3728	2.3799	2.3870	2.3940	2.4019
1987	2.4098	2.4178	2.4257	2.4336	2.4411	2.4486	2.4555	2.4624	2.4693	2.4768	2.4843	2.4918
1988	2.4987	2.5056	2.5125	2.5193	2.5262	2.5327	2.5391	2.5456	2.5537	2.5618	2.5708	2.5797
1989	2.5887	2.5983	2.6079	2.6175	2.6271	2.6367	2.6462	2.6564	2.6666	2.6768	2.6871	2.6979
1990	2.7088	2.7196	2.7304	2.7413	2.7521	2.7629	2.7738	2.7846	2.7954	2.8063	2.8171	2.8273
1991	2.8375	2.8477	2.8579	2.8675	2.8771	2.8861	2.8950	2.9033	2.9116	2.9200	2.9277	2.9354
1992	2.9431	2.9508	2.9585	2.9663	2.9740	2.9817	2.9894	2.9971	3.0048	3.0125	3.0202	3.0279

*The repayment supplement is based on figures at 5th of the month. These start in January 1975 and are the same in the official figures as at 1st of the month except where indicated, when the last digit is a "4", not a "3" (eg 2.0554, not 2.0553).

Remission of tax due

Extra-statutory concession A19 (as at 10 January 1992) - In certain circumstances arrears of tax are wholly or partly waived if they have arisen through the failure of the Department to make proper and timely use of information supplied by the taxpayer about his income and personal circumstances so that he could reasonably believe that his affairs were in order. The concession is not normally given where a taxpayer is notified of the arrear by the end of the tax year following that in which it arose. Both the reasonable belief and failure to make use of information conditions must be met.

The special scale for taxpayers either at least 65 years old or receiving a national retirement pension (or a widow's pension) on the notification date is shown in the right hand columns.

Date of notifying taxpayer or agent of arrears	Taxpayer's gross income £	Remission	Older tax-payer's gross income -£	Remission
6.4.82 (inc) to 21.4.83 (inc)	0 - 7,000 7,001* - 9,000 9,001 - 11,500 11,501 - 14,000 14,001 - 19,500 19,501 or more	All 75% 50% 25% 10% None	0 - 9,000 9,001 - 11,000 11,001 - 13,500 13,501 - 16,000 16,001 - 21,500 21,501 or more	All 75% 50% 25% 10% None
22.4.83 to 30.7.84	0 - 7,500 7,501 -9,500 9,501 - 12,000 12,001 - 14,500 14,501 - 20,500 20,501 or more	All 75% 50% 25% 10% None	0 - 9,500 9,501 - 11,500 11,501 - 14,000 14,001 - 16,500 16,501 - 22,500 22,501 or more	All 75% 50% 25% 10% None
31.7.84 to 22.7.85	0 - 8,000 8,001 - 10,000 10,001 - 12,500 12,501 - 15,000 15,001 - 21,500 21,501 or more	All 75% 50% 25% 10% None	0 - 10,500 10,501 - 12,500 12,501 - 15,000 15,001 - 17,500 17,501 - 24,000 24,001 or more	All 75% 50% 25% 10% None
23.7.85 to 13.3.90	0 - 8,500 8,501 - 10,500 10,501 - 13,500 13,501 - 16,000 16,001 - 23,000 23,001 or more	All 75% 50% 25% 10% None	0 - 11,000 11,001 - 13,000 13,001 - 16,000 16,001 - 18,500 18,501 - 25,500 25,501 or more	All 75% 50% 25% 10% None
14.3.90 and after	0 - 12,000 12,001 - 14,500 14,501 - 18,500 18,501 - 22,000 22,001 - 32,000 32,001 or more	All 75% 50% 25% 10% None	0 - 15,300 15,301 - 17,800 17,801 - 21,800 21,801 - 25,300 25,301 - 35,300 35,301 or more	All 75% 50% 25% 10% None

* ie over £7,000

Inspectors of Taxes have discretion to give a measure of relief if the taxpayer's gross income marginally exceeds the limits set out above and he has large or exceptional family responsibilities. Prior to Independent Taxation (6 April 1990) income limits for the purposes of the concession applied equally to a single person or the joint incomes of a husband and wife. With the introduction of Independent Taxation, the income scale will apply only to the spouse assessed. The new rules apply to arrears of tax, the actual or likely amount of which is notified to a taxpayer on or after 6 April 1990. The concession also applies for CGT purposes.

Interest on overdue tax

Interest is charged at a prescribed rate on overdue ACT and IT on company payments (s 87 TMA 1970) and other overdue tax (s 86 TMA 1970). The same rate generally applies in investigation settlements (see s 88 TMA 1970). A different rate applies to IHT/CTT.

Summary

Tax overdue	IT (Scheds A, C, D and higher rate tax), CGT & CT	ACT	IT (Sched E)	IHT/CTT
Interest period starts ("the reckonable date")	On due date * (see overleaf) unless assessment appealed and application to postpone tax made, when reckonable date is for: *Tax not postponed:* the later of (a) original due date and (b) Table date (see overleaf) (or, if earlier 30 days after determination of application) *Tax postponed* (and additional tax): the later of (a) original due date and (b) Table date (or, if earlier, 30 days after issue of notice of total tax payable)	On due date	On 14th day after demand issued (or date shown in direct collection assessment)	On due date
Interest period ends	On date of payment			
Remission of interest	If less than £30 (or £10 on tax assessed pre-1.8.80) and Board of Inland Revenue thinks fit			N/A

* See ESC A17 when death of taxpayer before due date for payments due.

Prescribed rates

Period	%
1.12.82 - 30.4.85	8
1.5.85 - 5.8.86	11
6.8.86 - 5.11.86	8.5
6.11.86 - 5.4.87	9.5
6.4.87 - 5.6.87	9
6.6.87 - 5.9.87	8.25
6.9.87 - 5.12.87	9
6.12.87 - 5.5.88	8.25
6.5.88 - 5.8.88	7.75
6.8.88 - 5.10.88	9.75
6.10.88 - 5.1.89	10.75
6.1.89 - 5.7.89	11.5
6.7.89 - 5.11.89	12.25
6.11.89 - 5.11.90	13
6.11.90 - 5.3.91	12.25
6.3.91 - 5.5.91	11.50
6.5.91 - 5.7.91	10.75
6.7.91 - 5.10.91	10
6.10.91 -	9.25

IHT

Period	%
1.12.82 - 30.4.85	6 or 8*
1.5.85 - 15.12.86	9 or 11*
16.12.86 - 5.6.87	8
6.6.87 - 5.8.88	6
6.8.88 - 5.10.88	8
6.10.88 - 5.7.89	9
6.7.89 - 5.3.91	11
6.3.91 - 5.5.91	10
6.5.91 - 5.7.91	9
6.7.91 -	8

* Pre-16.12.86 lower rate applied on death etc.

Repayment supplements

Tax free simple interest is paid on certain delayed repayments of taxes after 31.7.75. (For IHT, the interest rate on overpaid tax is the same as for underpaid tax and runs from the date of over-payment.)

Summary

	Persons (other than companies)	Companies
Tax repaid	Principally IT or CGT	CT(ACT), IT or tax credits
Amount repaid	£25 or more	£100 or more
Minimum delay	Over 12 months from relevant year of assessment	Over 12 months from 'material date' (broadly, last date when CT due for relevant accounting period)
Interest period starts ('the relevant time/date')	At end of above-mentioned 12 months (or, if overpaid later, at end of year of assessment in which overpaid)	On the anniversary of material date (or, if overpaid later, the anniversary of material date next occurring)
Interest period ends	End of tax month in which repayment order issued	

Rates

Tax month/s	%
6.12.82 - 5.5.85	8
6.5.85 - 5.8.86	11
6.8.86 - 5.11.86	8.5
6.11.86 - 5.4.87	9.5
6.4.87 - 5.6.87	9
6.6.87 - 5.9.87	8.25
6.9.87 - 5.12.87	9
6.12.87 - 5.5.88	8.25
6.5.88 - 5.8.88	7.75
6.8.88 - 5.10.88	9.75
6.10.88 - 5.1.89	10.75
6.1.89 - 5.7.89	11.5
6.7.89 - 5.11.89	12.25
6.11.89 - 5.11.90	13
6.11.90 - 5.3.91	12.25
6.3.91 - 5.5.91	11.50
6.5.91 - 5.7.91	10.75
6.7.91 - 5.10.91	10
6.10.91 -	9.25

Double Tax Agreements
List of all UK agreements (including terminated agreements)

Country	SI (or SR&O) No	Entry into force date (if after 5.4.70 or 12.3.75 (CT))
Algeria		
Agreement of 27.5.81		
(Air transport profits)	1984/362	14.3.84
Antigua & Barbuda		
Arrangement of 19.12.47	1947/2865	
Amending agreement of 5.3.68	1968/1096	
Argentina		
Agreement of 28.7.49		
(Shipping and air transport profits)	1949/1435	
(A comprehensive Convention agreed at official level in December 1980.)		
Aruba - see Netherlands Antilles		
Australia		
Agreement of 7.12.67	1968/305	
Amending Protocol of 29.1.80	1980/707	21.5.80
(Discussion on revision began February 1984.)		
Austria		
Convention of 20.7.56*	1957/598	
Convention of 30.4.69	1970/1947	17.12.70
Amending Protocol of 17.11.77	1979/117	6.2.79
Bahrain		
(Agreement at official level in March 1985 on the text of an air transport profits agreement.)		
Bangladesh		
Convention of 8.8.79	1980/708	8.7.80
Barbados		
Arrangement of 4.3.49*	1949/358	
Agreement of 26.3.70	1970/952	26.6.70
Amending Protocol of 18.9.73	1973/2096	12.12.73
Belgium		
Convention of 27.3.49*	1954/487	
Convention of 29.8.67*	1970/636	28.4.70
Convention of 1.6.87	1987/2053	21.10.89
Belize		
Arrangement of 19.12.47	1947/2866	
Amending Arrangement of 8.4.68	1968/573	
Amending Arrangement of 12.12.73	1973/2097	12.12.73
Botswana		
Arrangement of 25.11.49*	1949/2198	
Amending Agreement of 9.4.70*	1970/953	26.6.70
Agreement of 5.10.77	1978/183	9.2.78
Brazil		
Agreement of 29.12.67		
(Shipping and air transport profits)	1968/572	
(There were discussions about a comprehensive Convention in January 1977.)		
Brunei		
Arrangement of 8.12.50	1950/1977	
Amending Arrangement of 4.3.68	1968/306	
Amending Arrangement of 12.12.73	1973/2098	12.12.73
Bulgaria		
Convention of 16.9.87	1987/2054	28.12.87
Burma (now Myanmar)		
Agreement of 13.3.50	1952/751	
Amending Protocol of 4.4.51	1952/751	
Cameroon		
Agreement of 22.4.82 (Air transport profits)	1982/1841	31.3.86
Canada		
Agreement of 6.11.46 (Capital Taxes)*	1946/1884	
Agreement of 12.12.66*	1967/482	
Convention of 8.9.78	1980/709	17.12.80
Amending Protocol of 15.4.80	1980/1528	18.12.80
Amending Protocol of 16.10.85	1985/1996	23.12.85
Dividend and Interest Regulations of 4.6.80	1980/780	1.7.80

Country	SI No	Date of entry into force
Amending Dividend Regulations	1987/2071	1.1.88
China		
Agreement of 10.3.81		
(Air transport profits and employees)	1981/1119	4.9.81
Agreement of 26.7.84	1984/1826	23.12.84
Cyprus		
Arrangement of 8.8.47*	1947/1774	
Amending Agreement of 7.3.68*	1968/1097	
Amending Agreement of 18.5.73*	1973/1325	6.8.73
Convention of 20.6.74	1975/425	18.3.75
Amending Protocol of 2.4.80	1980/1529	15.12.80
Czechoslovakia		
Convention of 5.11.90	1991/2876	20.12.91
Denmark		
Convention of 27.3.50*	1950/1195	
Amending Protocol of 7.7.66*	1967/163	
Amending Protocol of 18.12.68*	1969/1068	
Amending Protocol of 8.2.73*	1973/1326	10.8.73
Convention of 11.11.80	1980/1960	17.12.80
Amending Protocol of 1.7.91	1991/2877	19.12.91
Dominica		
Arrangement of 4.3.49*	1949/359	
Amending Agreement of 7.3.68*	1968/1098	
(A new Agreement is under consideration.)		
Egypt		
Convention of 25.4.77	1980/1091	23.8.80
Ethiopia		
Agreement of 1.2.77		
(Air transport profits)	1977/1297	12.7.78
Falkland Islands		
Arrangement of 4.3.49*	1949/360	
Amending Arrangement of 8.4.68*	1968/575	
Amending Arrangement of 18.12.74*	1974/2149	18.12.74
Arrangement of 14.3.84	1984/363	27.6.84
Faroe Islands (see also Denmark)		
Danish Convention of 27.3.50	1950/1195	
Extension of 31.10.60	1961/579	
Danish Amending Protocol of 7.7.66*	1967/163	
Extension of 24.10.67*	1968/307	
Danish Amending Protocol of 18.12.68*	1969/1068	31.5.71
Extension of 27.11.70	1971/717	31.5.71
Danish Amending Protocol of 8.2.73*	1973/1326	19.12.75
Extension of 7.3.75	1975/2190	19.12.75
Fiji		
Arrangement of 10.5.50*	1950/749	
Amending Arrangement of 4.3.68*	1968/308	
Convention of 21.11.75	1976/1342	17.8.76
Finland		
Convention of 17.7.69	1970/153	
Amending Protocol of 17.5.73*	1973/1327	27.6.74
Amending Protocol of 16.11.79	1980/710	25.4.81
Amending Protocol of 1.10.85	1985/1997	20.2.87
Amending Protocol of 26.9.91	1991/2878	23.12.91
France		
Convention of 21.6.63 (Capital Taxes)	1963/1319	
Convention of 22.5.68	1968/1869	
Amending Protocol of 10.2.71*	1971/718	7.5.71
Amending Protocol of 14.5.73	1973/1328	6.8.73
Amending Protocol of 12.6.86	1987/466	7.4.87
Amending Protocol of 15.10.87	1987/2055	23.12.87
(Discussions at official level on new comprehensive Agreement)		
Gabon		
(There were discussions at official level during March 1986 concerning a comprehensive Agreement.)		

Gambia
Arrangement of 19.12.47*	1947/2867	
Amending Agreement of 1.4.68*	1968/1099	
Convention of 20.5.80	1980/1963	5.7.82

German Democratic Republic
(See German Federal Republic with effect from 1.1.91)

German Federal Republic
Convention of 26.11.64	1967/25	
Amending Protocol of 23.3.70	1971/874	1.6.71

(Agreement at official level in January 1975 to an Amending Protocol which now needs to be updated. Discussions to be held on new comprehensive Agreement.)

Ghana
Arrangement of 19.12.47	1947/2868	
Convention of 29.11.77 was never ratified by Ghana – see Inland Revenue Press Release dated 31.1.91.	1978/785	

(Agreement at official level on text of a comprehensive agreement)

Greece
Convention of 25.6.53	1954/142	

Grenada
Arrangement of 4.3.49	1949/361	
Amending Agreement of 25.7.68	1968/1867	

Guernsey
Arrangement of 24.6.52	1952/1215	

(There were exploratory talks in 1978 about a possible revision.)

Guyana
Arrangement of 8.8.47*	1947/1773	

(Agreement at official level on text of a comprehensive agreement)

Hungary
Agreement of 5.6.75 (Air transport profits and employees)*	1975/2189	19.1.76
Convention of 28.11.77	1978/1056	27.8.78

Iceland
Agreement of 27.4.28 (Shipping profits)*	1928/563	
Convention of 30.9.91	1991/2879	19.12.91

India
Agreement of 3.4.56 (Capital Taxes)	1956/998	
Convention of 16.4.81	1981/1120	21.10.81

(Agreement at official level on text of a comprehensive agreement)

Indonesia
Agreement of 13.3.74	1975/2191	3.1.76

(Discussions about a new Agreement commenced in September 1983.)

Iran
Agreement of 21.12.60 (Air transport profits)	1960/2419	

Irish Republic
Agreement of 14.4.26*		
Amending Agreement of 25.4.28*	TA 1970	
Supplementary Agreement of 4.4.59* }	Sch 12	
Supplementary Agreement of 23.6.60*		
Amending Agreement of 2.5.73*	FA 1973 Sch 17 F(No 2)A	20.9.73
Amending Agreement of 3.6.75*	1975 Sch 11	23.9.75
Agreement of 18.5.49 (Profits tax and corporation tax)*	1949/1434	
Amending Protocol of 2.5.73*	1973/1331	4.8.73
Convention of 2.6.76	1976/2151	23.12.76
Amending Protocol of 28.10.76	1976/2152	23.12.76
Convention of 7.12.77 (Capital Taxes)	1978/1107	2.10.78

Isle of Man
Arrangement of 29.7.55	1955/1205	
Amending Arrangement of 4.11.91	1991/2880	19.12.91

Israel
Convention of 26.9.62	1963/616	
Amending Protocol of 20.4.70	1971/391	25.3.71

Italy
Convention of 4.7.60*	1962/2787	
Exchange of Notes of 4.7.60*	1962/2787	
Convention of 15.2.66 (Capital Taxes)	1968/304	
Amending Protocol of 28.4.69*	1973/1763	5.11.73
Convention of 21.10.88	1990/2590	31.12.90

Ivory Coast
Convention of 26.6.85	1987/169	10.2.87

Jamaica
Agreement of 2.4.65*	1965/1537	

Japan (continued from top of right column)
Amending Agreement of 9.5.69*	1969/1069	
Agreement of 16.3.73	1973/1329	31.12.73

Japan
Convention of 4.9.62*	1963/887	
Convention of 10.2.69	1970/1948	25.12.70
Exchange of Notes of 10.2.69	1970/1948	25.12.70
Amending Protocol of 14.2.80	1980/1530	31.10.80

Jersey
Arrangement of 24.6.52	1952/1216	

(There were exploratory talks in 1978 about a possible revision.)

Jordan
Agreement of 6.3.78 (Shipping and air transport profits)	1979/300	7.2.80

Kenya
Arrangement of 24.6.52*	1952/1214	
Agreement of 31.7.73 }		
Amending Protocol of 20.1.76 }	1977/1299	18.10.77
Exchange of Notes of 8.2.77 }		

Kiribati and Tuvalu
Arrangement of 10.5.50	1950/750	
Amending Arrangement of 4.3.68	1968/309	
Amending Arrangement of 25.7.74	1974/1271	25.7.74

Korea
Convention of 21.4.77	1978/786	31.5.78
Amending Protocol of 21.4.77	1978/786	31.5.78

Kuwait
Agreement of 25.9.84 (Air transport profits)	1984/1825	8.4.85

Lebanon
Agreement of 26.2.64 (Shipping and air transport profits)	1964/278	

Lesotho
Arrangement of 25.11.49	1949/2197	
Amending Agreement of 3.7.68	1968/1868	

Luxembourg
Convention of 24.5.67	1968/1100	
Amending Protocol of 18.7.78	1980/567	21.5.80
Amending Protocol of 28.1.83	1984/364	19.3.84

Malawi
Agreement of 25.11.55	1956/619	
Amending Agreement of 1.4.64	1964/1401	
Amending Agreement of 2.4.68	1968/1101	
Amending Agreement of 10.2.78	1979/302	14.3.79

Malaysia
Agreement of 30.8.63*	1967/1925	
Amending Agreement of 17.7.67*	1967/1925	
Agreement of 30.3.73	1973/1330	13.9.73
Amending Protocol of 30.3.73	1973/1330	13.9.73
Amending Protocol of 21.7.87	1987/2056	26.1.88

Malta
Arrangement of 28.3.62	1962/639	
Amending Agreement of 29.11.74	1975/426	18.3.75

(Discussions at official level to be held in April 1991 to review the Arrangement.)

Mauritius
Arrangement of 8.8.47*	1947/1775	
Convention of 11.2.81	1981/1121	19.10.81
Amending Protocol of 23.10.86	1987/467	

Mexico
(Agreement at official level on text of a comprehensive agreement)

Montserrat
Arrangement of 19.12.47	1947/2869	
Amending Arrangement of 8.4.68	1968/576	

(There were discussions about amending arrangements in 1971.)

Morocco
Convention of 8.9.81	1991/2881	29.11.90

Namibia (S. W. Africa)
S African Convention of 28.5.62	1962/2352	
Extension of 8.8.62	1962/2788	
S African Amending Protocol of 14.6.67	1967/1489	
Extension of 14.6.67	1967/1490	

Netherlands
Convention of 15.10.48 (Capital Taxes)*	1950/1197	
Convention of 31.10.67*	1968/577	
Amending Protocol of 22.3.77*	1977/1300	22.9.77
Convention of 11.12.79 (Capital Taxes)	1980/706	16.6.80
Convention of 7.11.80	1980/1961	6.4.81

41

Amending Protocol of 12.7.83	1983/1902	20.12.90
Dividend Regulations of 18.7.67*	1967/1063	
Amending Protocol of 24.8.89	1990/2152	20.12.90

Netherlands Antilles and Aruba

Netherlands Convention of 31.10.67*	1968/577	18.1.71
Extension of 24.7.70*	1970/1949	18.1.71

(There are no immediate plans to hold further discussions
on a new agreement.)

New Zealand

Agreement of 13.6.66*	1966/1020	
Amending Protocol of 25.3.80*	1980/1531	17.11.80
Convention of 4.8.83	1984/365	16.3.84
Exchange of Notes of 22.12.83	1984/365	16.3.84

Nigeria

Arrangement of 19.12.47*	1947/2878	
Agreement of 9.6.87	1987/2057	27.12.87

Norway

Convention of 22.1.69*	1970/154	
Amending Protocol of 23.6.77*	1979/303	22.6.79
Second Amending Protocol of 29.3.78*	1979/118	6.2.79
Exchange of Notes of 5.5.78*	1979/303	22.6.79
Third amending Protocol of 16.10.79*	1980/711	2.12.80
Fourth amending Protocol of 16.10.79*	1980/712	3.12.80
Fifth amending Protocol of 30.9.80*	1980/1962	7.9.82
Convention of 3.10.85	1985/1998	20.12.85

Oman

(Agreement reached at official level in March 1985
on the text of an air transport profits agreement.)

Pakistan

Agreement of 8.6.57 (Capital Taxes)	1957/1522	
Agreement of 24.4.61*	1961/2467	
Convention of 24.11.86	1987/2058	8.12.87

Papua New Guinea

Convention of 17.9.91	1991/2882	20.12.91

Peru

(Negotiations for a comprehensive Convention began in July 1981.)

Philippines

Convention of 10.6.76	1978/184	9.2.78

Poland

Convention of 16.12.76	1978/282	25.2.78

Portugal

Convention of 27.3.68	1969/599	

Qatar

(Agreement reached at official level in March 1985 on the text
of an air transport profits agreement.)

Romania

Convention of 18.9.75	1977/57	17.1.77
Exchange of Notes of 3.2.76	1977/57	17.1.77

Saudi Arabia

(Agreement at official level on text of an air agreement)

St Christopher (St Kitts) & Nevis

Arrangement of 19.12.47	1947/2872	

St Lucia

Arrangement of 4.3.49*	1949/366	
Amending Agreement of 5.4.68*	1968/1102	

(Terminated with effect in St Lucia from 1.1.88 and in the UK
from 6.4.88 (income tax) or 1.4.88 (corporation tax). A new
Agreement is under consideration.)

St Vincent & Grenadines

Arrangement of 4.3.49*	1949/367	
Amending Agreement of 1.4.68*	1968/1103	

(A new Agreement is under consideration.)

Seychelles

Arrangement of 8.8.47*	1947/1778	
Amending Arrangement of 18.3.69*	1969/379	
Amending Arrangement of 25.7.74*	1974/1272	25.7.74

Sierra Leone

Arrangement of 19.12.47	1947/2873	
Amending Agreement of 18.3.68	1968/1104	

Singapore

Agreement of 1.12.66 }	1967/483	
Amending Protocol of 21.7.75 }		
Exchange of Notes of 27.12.75 }		
Exchange of Notes of 12.3.76	1978/787	4.8.78
Exchange of Notes of 23.7.77		

Solomon Islands

Arrangement of 10.5.50	1950/748	
Amending Arrangement of 8.4.68	1968/574	
Amending Arrangement of 25.7.74	1974/1270	25.7.74

South Africa

Agreement of 14.10.46 (Capital Taxes)*	1947/314	
Amending Agreement of 22.12.54		
(Capital Taxes)*	1955/424	
Convention of 21.11.68	1969/864	
Convention of 31.7.78 (Capital Taxes)	1979/576	6.5.79

Spain

Agreement of 21.12.68		
(Air transport profits)*	1969/378	
Convention of 21.10.75	1976/1919	25.11.76

Sri Lanka

Convention of 21.6.79	1980/713	21.5.80
Exchange of Notes of 13.2.80	1980/713	21.5.80

Sudan

Convention of 8.3.75	1977/1719	25.10.77

Swaziland

Agreement of 26.11.68	1969/380	

Sweden

Convention of 28.7.60*	1961/577	
Convention of 14.10.64 (Capital Taxes)*	1965/599	
Amending Protocol of 25.3.66*	1968/1105	
Amending Protocol of 27.6.68*	1968/2034	
Amending Protocol of 27.9.73*	1974/558	26.3.74
Amending Protocol of 6.6.79*	1980/1532	3.12.80
Convention of 8.10.80 (Capital Taxes)	1981/840	19.6.81
Convention of 30.8.83	1984/366	26.3.84
Dividend Regulations of 28.3.61	1961/619	
Amending Protocol of 21.12.87		
(Capital taxes)	1989/986	17.3.86

Switzerland

Agreement of 17.10.31 (Agency profits)*	1932/925	
Convention of 30.9.54*	1955/422	
Convention of 12.6.56 (Capital Taxes)	1957/426	
Amending Protocol of 14.6.66*	1967/26	
Amending Protocol of 2.8.74*	1975/1043	25.6.75
Convention of 8.12.77	1978/1408	7.10.78
Amending Protocol of 5.3.81	1982/714	18.5.82

(The text of an Amending Protocol was agreed at
official level in August 1985. Also, agreement has been reached at
official level on the text of a new capital taxes Convention.)

Tanzania

Arrangement of 24.6.52 (Tanganyika)*	1952/1212	
Arrangement of 24.6.52 (Zanzibar)*	1952/1211	

(There were discussions about a new comprehensive Convention
in February 1977 before the arrangements were terminated.)

Thailand

Convention of 18.2.81	1981/1546	20.11.81

Trinidad & Tobago

Agreement of 29.12.66*	1967/484	
Amending Protocol of 10.12.69*	1970/483	
Amending Protocol of 15.1.71*	1971/2117	31.12.71
Convention of 31.12.82	1983/1903	22.12.83

Tunisia

Convention of 15.12.82	1984/133	8.2.84

Turkey

Agreement of 19.2.86	1988/932	26.10.88

Uganda

Arrangement of 24.6.52	1952/1213	

(Agreement reached in March 1985 on the text of a new
comprehensive Convention.)

Union of Soviet Socialist Republics (under review)

Agreement of 3.5.74 (Air transport profits		
and employees)	1974/1269	29.9.74
Convention of 31.7.85	1986/224	12.2.86

United Arab Emirates

(Agreement reached at official level in March 1985 on the
text of an air transport profits agreement.)

United States of America

Convention of 16.4.45*	1946/1327	
Convention of 16.4.45 (Capital Taxes)*	1946/1351	
Amending Protocol of 6.6.46*	1946/1327	
Amending Protocol of 25.5.54*	1955/162	
Amending Protocol of 19.8.57*	1958/1751	
Amending Protocol of 17.3.66*	1966/1188	

(As to retrospective termination, see TA 1988 Sch 30 para 14.)

Convention of 31.12.75 }		
Exchange of Notes of 13.4.76 }		
Amending Protocol of 26.8.76 }	1980/568	25.4.80
Amending Protocol of 31.3.77		

(Discussions about Amending Protocol resumed in Sept 1986.)

Convention of 19.10.78 (Capital Taxes)	1979/1454	11.11.79
Amending Protocol of 15.3.79	1980/568	25.4.80
Dividend Regulations of 2.8.46	1946/1331	
Amending Dividend Reg'ns of 31.3.55	1955/499	
Amending Dividend Reg'ns of 25.5.61	1961/985	
Amending Dividend Reg'ns of 22.5.80	1980/779	22.5.80

Venezuela
Agreement of 8.3.78		
(Shipping and air transport profits)	1979/301	8.6.87
Amending Protocol of 23.11.87	1988/933	27.10.88
(Agreement at official level on text of a comprehensive agreement)

Virgin Islands
| Arrangement of 19.12.47* | 1947/2874 | |
| Amending Arrangement of 8.4.68* | 1968/578 | |
(A new Agreement agreed in outline in 1972.)

Yugoslavia
| Convention of 6.11.81 | 1981/1815 | 16.9.82 |

Zaire
| Agreement of 11.10.76 (Shipping | | |
| and air transport profits) | 1977/1298 | 1.3.78 |

Zambia
Agreement of 25.11.55*	1956/619	
Amending Agreement of 23.3.64*	1964/1402	
Amending Agreement of 6.4.68*	1968/1106	
Convention of 22.3.72	1972/1721	29.3.73
Amending Protocol of 30.4.81	1981/1816	14.1.83

Zimbabwe
Agreement of 25.11.55*	1956/619	
Amending Agreement of 23.7.64*	1965/142	
Convention of 19.10.82	1982/1842	11.2.83
(Discussions about an Amending Protocol are planned.)

European Community
Convention of 23.7.90
(also joint and unilateral Declarations)

Air & Shipping Transport profits: There are air only agreements (details are in the above list) with Algeria, Cameroon, China, Ethiopia, Iran, Kuwait and the USSR. There are shipping and air agreements with Argentina, Brazil, Jordan, Lebanon, Venezuela and Zaire.

Capital Taxes: There are agreements with France, India, Ireland, Italy, Netherlands, Pakistan, South Africa, Sweden, Switzerland and the USA.

* These agreements have been terminated.

Exchange Rates

The following "units per £1" rates are used for double tax relief purposes, and generally.

Exchange rates year end:

	31 March 1988	1989	30 Mar 1990	28 Mar 1991	31 Dec 1987	30 Dec 1988	29 Dec 1989	31 Dec 1990
Australia (A$)	2.54	2.061	2.1830	2.2380	2.60	2.116	2.0413	2.5000
Austria (S)	21.93	22.415	19.605	20.785	20.88	22.555	19.185	20.270
Belgium (Fr)	65.40	66.85	57.800	61.200	62.11	67.400	57.400	59.750
Canada (Can $)	2.33	2.016	1.9270	2.0110	2.44	2.154	1.8675	2.2400
Denmark (Kr)	11.93	12.433	10.643	11.400	11.42	12.41	10.610	11.150
France (Fr)	10.60	10.793	9.3525	10.055	10.03	10.958	9.3300	9.8200
Germany (DM)	3.13	3.198	2.7800	2.9650	2.96	3.208	2.7275	2.8850
Hong Kong (HK $)	14.70	13.145	12.856	13.544	14.60	14.116	12.584	15.045
Irish Republic (IR £)	1.17	1.199	1.0420	1.1130	1.12	1.202	1.0360	1.0860
Italy (Li)	2,318	2,344	2,048	2,207	2,188	2,362	2,045	2,177
Japan (Yen)	234.25	223.50	259.25	245.50	227.79	226	231.75	261.75
Luxembourg (f)	-	66.850	57.800	61.200	-	67.400	57.400	59.750
Netherlands (f)	3.51	3.605	3.1325	3.3425	3.33	3.623	3.0825	3.2550
Norway (Kr)	11.78	11.61	10.813	11.555	11.70	11.878	10.635	11.348
Portugal (Esc)	255.75	263.10	246.00	261.40	245.70	264.50	241.20	255.30
South Africa (R) (Com)	3.99	4.322	4.3675	4.7520	3.62	4.304	4.1088	4.9373
(Fin. rate)	-	7.030	6.5849	5.6975	-	6.959	5.7053	6.5765
Spain (Ptas)	208.33	199.05	177.95	182.95	202.02	204.75	176.00	183.70
Sweden (Kr)	11.09	10.858	10.088	10.720	10.87	11.08	9.9850	10.865
Switzerland (Fr)	2.58	2.805	2.4625	2.5300	2.39	2.718	2.4875	2.4600
USA ($)	1.89	1.688	1.6475	1.7390	1.88	1.809	1.6125	1.9300

Average exchange rates for the year ending:

	31 March 1988	1989	1990	1991	31 December 1987	1988	1989	1990
Algeria (Dinar)	8.13	10.796	12.097	22.010	7.63	10.315	11.100	15.402
Argentina (Austral from 15.6.85)	4.31	28.363	2,893	12,864	3.086	16.183	491.63	8,702
Australia (A$)	2.39	2.19	2.1174	2.4342	2.35	2.28	2.0687	2.3533
Austria (Schilling)	20.96	22.809	20.472	20.446	20.66	28.951	21.603	20.214
Bahamas (B$)	-	-	-	-	-	-	-	-
Bahrain (Dinar)	0.641	0.665	0.6723	0.6981	0.617	0.672	0.7068	0.6698
Bangladesh (Taka)-	-	-	-	63.085	-	-	-	59.202
Barbados (BD $)	3.42	3.544	3.1160	3.7596	3.29	3.589	3.0487	3.5923
Belgium (Franc)	62.11	67.95	60.943	59.932	60.98	65.382	64.494	59.429
Bolivia (Boliviano from 1.1.87)	3.57	4.362	4.4667	6.2398	3.31	4.258	4.0302	5.6584
Botswana (Pula)	-	-	-	3.4124	-	-	-	3.2877
Brazil								
(Cruzado from 1.3.86 to 19.1.89)	80	1,159	-	-	49.02	460.33	-	-
(Cruzado from 23.1.89)	-	1.74	21.812	279.58	-	-	3.9895	123.62
Brunei ($)	-	-	3.1242	-	-	-	3.1878	-
Burma (Kyat)	10.83	11.367	10.290	11.335	10.64	11.263	10.197	11.043
Burundi (Burundi Franc)	-	-	-	308.44	-	-	-	301.55
Canada (Can $)	2.22	2.168	1.9246	2.1636	2.17	2.192	1.9371	2.0810
Cayman Islands (CI $)	-	-	-	1.5281	-	-	-	1.4725
Chile (Peso)	387.6	440.67	427.79	605.98	355.87	440.21	393.66	545.12
China (Renminbi yuan)	-	-	-	8.9861	-	-	-	8.4060
Colombia (Peso)	429.18	576.35	647.81	1012	393.7	532.67	570.27	889.32
Costa Rica (Colon)	-	-	-	178.79	-	-	-	161.88
Cuba (Cuban peso)	-	-	-	1.4629	-	-	-	1.4097
Cyprus (Cyprus pound)	-	-	-	0.8248	-	-	-	0.8121
Czechoslovakia (Koruna)	-	-	-	36.856	-	-	-	30.810
Denmark (Kroner)	11.39	12.528	11.282	11.150	11.194	11.972	11.969	11.005
Egypt (£)	2.88	4.122	4.0572	5.4187	1.93	4.074	3.8777	4.8434
Ecuador (Sucre)	-	-	-	1570	-	-	-	1407
El Salvador (Colon)	-	-	-	12.214	-	-	-	11.279
Ethiopia (Birr)	-	-	-	3.7696	-	-	-	3.6329
Fiji Islands (F $)	-	-	-	2.6926	-	-	-	2.6223
Finland (Markka)	7.25	7.48	6.7413	6.9494	7.19	7.444	7.0221	6.8008
France (Franc)	10.02	10.979	9.8839	9.8382	9.80	10.507	10.448	9.6862
French Cty/Africa (CFA Franc)	-	-	-	487.62	-	-	-	482.46
French Pacific Islands (CFP Franc)	-	-	-	174.94	-	-	-	173.20
Gambia (Dalasi)	-	-	-	14.469	-	-	-	14.287
Germany (Deutschmark)	2.98	3.246	2.9144	2.9090	-2.94	3.124	3.0786	2.8749
Ghana (Cedi)	286.53	398.14	481.52	639.38	264.55	360.66	443.88	584.38
Greece (Drachma)	229.89	263.25	264.15	299.91	221.24	252.16	265.64	282.08
Grenada (EC $)	4.59	4.758	4.3975	5.0347	4.41	4.818	4.4147	4.8041
Guyana (G$) (to 10.3.91)	15.6	15.836	48.752	80.209	13.16	16.051	39.822	68.324
(from 11.3.91)	-	-	-	206.30	-	-	-	-
Honduras (Lempira)	-	-	-	9.2382	-	-	-	7.4674
Hong Kong (HK$)	13.26	13.755	12.725	14.536	12.74	13.898	12.648	13.889
Hungary (Forint)	-	-	-	119.56	-	-	-	111.95
Iceland (Krona)	64.94	84.288	97.584	105.74	63.29	76.556	93.188	103.89
India (Rupee)	21.88	25.929	27.130	34.030	21.01	24.691	26.427	31.094
Indonesia (Rupiah)	2,809	3,039	2,930	3,536	2,688	3,015	2,905	3,302
Iran (Rial)	118.76	122.54	116.16	123.51	116.55	122.05	118.07	120.87
Iraq (Dinar)	0.529	0.579	0.5344	0.5803	0.508	0.555	0.5236	0.5551
Irish Republic (IR £)	1.12	1.214	1.0963	1.0889	1.10	1.168	1.1552	1.0755
Israel (New Sheqel from 3.9.85)	2.7	3.008	3,1877	3.8222	2.6	2.85	3.1304	3.5954
Italy (Lire)	2,174	2,394	2,142	2,169	2,119	2,314	2,246	2,132
Jamaica (J$)	9.17	9.496	10.066	13.975	8.93	9.609	9.1307	12.630
Japan (Yen)	234.74	229.33	235.64	258.31	236.41	226.92	225.64	257.45
Jordan (Dinar)	0.575	0.802	1.0354	1.6195	0.552	0.669	0.9536	1.1758
Kenya (Shilling)	28.01	32.219	34.855	44.754	26.6	31.28	33.289	40.626
Korea South (Won)	-	-	-	1,310	-	-	-	1,247
Kuwait (Dinar)	0.474	0.50	0.4789	0.4977*	0.457	0.497	0.4807	0.4919†
Laos (New Kip)	-	-	-	1,301	-	-	-	1,262
Lebanon (LL)	380.23	804.21	851	1,660	252.53	731.23	813.85	1,254
Libya (Dinar)	0.495	0.509	0.4836	0.5143	0.488	0.508	0.4895	0.5047
Luxembourg (Franc)	-	67.950	60.943	59.932	-	65.382	64.494	59.429
Malawi (Kwacha)	4.58	4.4023	2.70	4.9407	4.507	4.4579	-	4.7805

* (From 1.3.90 to 30.7.90) † (From 1.1.90 to 30.7.90)

	31 March				31 December			
	1988	1989	1990	1991	1987	1988	1989	1990
Malaysia (Ringgit)	4.29	4.727	4.4021	5.0601	4.12	4.664	4.4287	4.8274
Malta (Lm)	0.571	0.59	0.5553	0.6381	0.561	0.586	0.5692	0.6612
Mauritius (Rupee)	21.74	24.472	24.477	26.851	20.79	23.626	24.598	26.100
Mexico (Peso)	2,688	4,061	4,290	5,461	2,123	4,046	4,069	5,081
Morocco (Dirham)	-	-	-	14.984	-	-	-	14.541
Nepal (Rupee)	-	-	-	54.026	-	-	-	50.571
Netherlands (Guilder)	3.36	3.657	3.2821	3.2784	3.31	3.515	3.4677	3.2394
Netherlands Antilles (Antilles Guilder)	-	-	-	3.2770	-	-	-	3.1600
New Zealand (NZ $)	2.74	2.766	2.7490	3.1231	2.75	2.717	2.7340	2.9857
Nicaragua (Cordoba to 3.3.91)	-	-	-	2,970,339	-	-	-	1,011,621
(Gold Cordoba from 4.3.91)	-	-	-	9.3075	-	-	-	-
Nigeria (Naira)	7.3	10.324	12.339	16.254	6.71	8.488	11.789	14.198
Norway (Krone)	11.16	11.778	10.989	11.324	11.01	11.412	11.303	11.137
Oman (Rial Omani)	0.654	0.678	0.6263	0.7199	0.630	0.686	0.6297	0.6873
Pakistan (Rupee)	29.33	32.756	34.106	40.744	28.09	31.834	33.265	38.374
Papua New Guinea (Kina)	-	-	-	1.7485	-	-	-	1.6798
Paraguay (Guarani to 31.3.89)	568.18	596.98	-	-	500.00	570.87	625.03	-
(Guarani from 1.4.89)	-	-	1,976	2,346	-	-	1,871	2,182
Peru (Inti to 6.3.89)	32.05	394.37	-	-	26.04	59.005	-	-
(Inti from 7.3.89 -31.12.90)	-	2,082	14,090	373,556	-	-	10,707	285,494
(New Sol from 1.1.91)	-	-	-	1.0531	-	-	-	-
Philippines (Peso)	34.4	36.286	34.811	47.781	32.89	36.418	34.370	41.977
Poland (Zloty)	-	-	-	17,528	-	-	-	16,877
Portugal (Escudo)	237.53	266.09	251.04	256.37	230.11	255.93	257.63	253.52
Qatar (Riyal)	6.13	6.416	5.9242	6.8086	5.95	6.463	5.9556	6.4998
Romania (Leu)	-	-	-	46.470	-	-	-	34.979
Rwanda (Rwanda Franc)	-	-	-	166.54	-	-	-	140.70
Saudi Arabia (Riyal)	6.37	6.597	6.0962	7.0150	6.13	6.677	6.1217	6.6961
Seychelles (S Rupee)	-	-	-	9.5214	-	-	-	9.3264
Sierra Leone (Leone)	47.62	63.242	136.98	324.19	51.81	53.549	90.970	262.86
Singapore (S$)	3.52	3.472	3.1174	3.2907	3.44	3.584	3.1893	3.2258
Solomon Islands (SI $)	-	-	-	4.6887	-	-	-	4.4488
Somali republic (So shillings)	-	-	-	2,880	-	-	-	1,787
South Africa (Rand) (Com. rate)	3.45	4.288	4.2726	4.8180	3.33	4.045	4.2893	4.5953
(Fin. rate)	-	6.563	6.1834	6.6071	-	5.936	6.5755	6.7211
Spain (Peseta)	202.84	208.27	185.85	181.80	202.02	207.20	193.72	181.04
Sri Lanka (Rupee)	50	57.319	62.354	74.691	47.62	56.308	58.613	71.060
Sudan (Sudan pound)	-	-	-	21.025	-	-	-	20.258
Surinam (S Guilder)	-	-	-	3.2757	-	-	-	3.1540
Swaziland (Lilangeni)	-	-	-	4.7525	-	-	-	4.5785
Sweden (Krona)	10.56	11.194	10.292	10.748	10.37	10.945	10.559	10.537
Switzerland (Franc)	2.46	2.77	2.5722	2.4766	2.44	2.603	2.6916	2.4685
Syria (Syrian pound)	-	-	-	38.398	-	-	-	36.991
Taiwan ($)	51.55	49.573	42.491	50.557	52.08	50.941	43.279	48.050
Tanzania (Shilling)	119.90	207.27	277.07	365.65	101.73	180.83	232.82	346.17
Thailand (Baht)	42.92	44.475	41.640	2.3427	41.67	44.702	41.850	2.2642
Tonga Islands (Pa Anga)	-	-	-	47.037	-	-	-	45.347
Trinidad & Tobago (TT$)	6.13	7.182	6.9219	7.9419	5.88	6.832	6.9486	7.5950
Tunisia (Dinar)	1.41	1.594	1.5170	1.6088	1.36	1.526	1.5577	1.5196
Turkey (Lira)	1,961	3,013	3,730	5,496	1,370	2,516	3,468	4,656
Uganda (Old Shilling to 17.5.87)	2,299	-	-	-	2,137	-	-	-
(New Shilling from 18.5.87)	100.70	257.63	500.38	959.32	98.04	186.98	358.68	763.82
Utd Arab Emirates (Dirham)	6.25	6.464	5.9737	6.8617	6.54	6.544	6.0009	6.5549
Uruguay (Peso/New Peso)	416.67	749.33	1,232	2,740	357.14	635.43	973.16	2,072
USA ($)	1.70	1.797	1.6305	1.8682	1.63	1.781	1.6387	1.7854
USSR (Rouble)	-	-	-	1.0529	-	-	-	1.0341
Venezuela (Bolivar)	49.75	63.784	68.201	95.129	44.44	59.442	64.652	84.511
Vietnam (Dong)	-	-	-	10,139	-	-	-	8,671
Yemen North (Yemen rial)	-	-	-	22.051	-	-	-	20.290
Yemen South (Yemen dinar)	-	-	-	0.8131	-	-	-	0.7320
Yugoslavia (Dinar) (to 21.1.90)	-	-	-	-	-	-	-	192,950
(From 22.1.90)	-	-	-	21.719	-	-	-	20.176
Zaire Republic (Zaire)	202.02	430.94	704.71	3,066	168.63	324.69	604.34	1,145
Zambia (Kwacha)	14.06	15.851	32.779	83.316	15.77	14.25	21.884	65.793
Zimbabwe (Z$)	2.86	3.365	3.6523	4.8860	2.71	3.225	3.4642	4.3777
European Currency Unit (ECU)	1.47*	1.536	1.3760	1.4099	1.42	1.504	1.4208	1.3955

Retail Prices Index

	1950	1951	1952	1953	1954	1955	1956	1957	1958	1959
January	8.29	8.57	9.68	10.11	10.27	10.70	11.25	11.74	12.17	12.42
February	8.29	8.64	9.76	10.19	10.27	10.70	11.25	11.74	12.09	12.40
March	8.29	8.72	9.76	10.27	10.34	10.70	11.38	11.71	12.19	12.40
April	8.37	8.87	9.91	10.34	10.42	10.77	11.56	11.76	12.32	12.32
May	8.37	9.10	9.91	10.27	10.34	10.77	11.53	11.76	12.29	12.27
June	8.37	9.18	10.11	10.34	10.42	11.00	11.51	11.89	12.40	12.29
July	8.37	9.23	10.11	10.34	10.62	11.00	11.48	11.99	12.19	12.40
August	8.29	9.30	10.04	10.27	10.57	10.93	11.51	11.96	12.19	12.29
September	8.37	9.38	9.96	10.27	10.49	11.00	11.48	11.94	12.19	12.22
October	8.44	9.46	10.11	10.27	10.57	11.15	11.56	12.04	12.29	12.29
November	8.52	9.46	10.11	10.27	10.62	11.28	11.58	12.12	12.34	12.37
December	8.52	9.53	10.11	10.27	10.62	11.28	11.63	12.17	12.40	12.40

	1960	1961	1962	1963	1964	1965	1966	1967	1968	1969
January	12.37	12.62	13.21	13.56	13.84	14.47	15.11	15.67	16.07	17.06
February	12.37	12.62	13.23	13.69	13.84	14.47	15.11	15.67	16.15	17.16
March	12.34	12.67	13.28	13.71	13.89	14.52	15.13	15.67	16.20	17.21
April	12.40	12.75	13.46	13.74	14.02	14.80	15.34	15.79	16.50	17.41
May	12.40	12.78	13.51	13.74	14.14	14.85	15.44	15.79	16.50	17.39
June	12.47	12.90	13.59	13.74	14.20	14.90	15.49	15.84	16.58	17.47
July	12.50	12.90	13.54	13.66	14.20	14.90	15.41	15.74	16.58	17.47
August	12.42	13.00	13.43	13.61	14.25	14.93	15.51	15.72	16.60	17.41
September	12.42	13.00	13.41	13.66	14.25	14.93	15.49	15.69	16.63	17.47
October	12.52	13.00	13.41	13.71	14.27	14.96	15.51	15.82	16.70	17.59
November	12.60	13.16	13.46	13.74	14.37	15.01	15.61	15.92	16.76	17.64
December	12.62	13.18	13.51	13.76	14.42	15.08	15.64	16.02	16.96	17.77

	1970	1971	1972	1973	1974	1975	1976	1977	1978	1979
January	17.90	19.42	21.01	22.64	25.35	30.39	37.49	43.70	48.03	52.52
February	18.00	19.54	21.12	22.79	25.78	30.90	37.97	44.13	48.31	52.95
March	18.10	19.70	21.19	22.92	26.00	31.51	38.17	44.56	48.62	53.38
April	18.38	20.13	21.39	23.35	26.89	32.72	38.91	45.70	49.33	54.30
May	18.43	20.25	21.50	23.52	27.28	34.09	39.34	46.06	49.61	54.73
June	18.48	20.38	21.62	23.65	27.55	34.75	39.54	46.54	49.99	55.67
July	18.63	20.51	21.70	23.75	27.81	35.11	39.62	46.59	50.22	58.07
August	18.61	20.53	21.88	23.83	27.83	35.31	40.18	46.82	50.54	58.53
September	18.71	20.56	22.00	24.03	28.14	35.61	40.71	47.07	50.75	59.11
October	18.91	20.66	22.31	24.51	28.69	36.12	41.44	47.28	50.98	59.72
November	19.04	20.79	22.38	24.69	29.20	36.55	42.03	47.50	51.33	60.25
December	19.16	20.89	22.48	24.87	29.63	37.01	42.59	47.76	51.76	60.68

	1980	1981	1982	1983	1984	1985	1986	1987	1988	1989
January	62.18	70.29	78.73	82.61	86.84	91.20	96.25	100.00	103.30	111.00
February	63.07	70.93	78.76	82.97	87.20	91.94	96.60	100.40	103.70	111.80
March	63.93	71.99	79.44	83.12	87.48	92.80	96.73	100.60	104.10	112.30
April	66.11	74.07	81.04	84.28	88.64	94.78	97.67	101.80	105.80	114.30
May	66.72	74.55	81.62	84.64	88.97	95.21	97.85	101.90	106.20	115.00
June	67.35	74.98	81.85	84.84	89.20	95.41	97.79	101.90	106.60	115.40
July	67.91	75.31	81.88	85.30	89.10	95.23	97.52	101.80	106.70	115.50
August	68.06	75.87	81.90	85.68	89.94	95.49	97.82	102.10	107.90	115.80
September	68.49	76.30	81.85	86.06	90.11	95.44	98.30	102.40	108.40	116.60
October	68.92	76.98	82.26	86.36	90.67	95.59	98.45	102.90	109.50	117.50
November	69.48	77.79	82.66	86.67	90.95	95.92	99.29	103.40	110.00	118.50
December	69.86	78.28	82.51	86.89	90.87	96.05	99.62	103.30	110.30	118.80

	1990	1991	1992	1993
January	119.50	130.20	135.60	137.9
February	120.20	130.90	136.30	138.8
March	121.40	131.40	136.70	
April	125.10	133.10		160.6
May	126.20	133.50	139.3	141.1
June	126.70	134.10	139.3	
July	126.80	133.80	138.8	
August	128.10	134.10	138.9	
September	129.30	134.60	139.4	
October	130.30	135.10		
November	130.00	135.60	139.7	
December	129.90	135.70		

Notes: The RPI figure for December 1947 was 7.63; for December 1948, 7.98; and for December 1949, 8.29.
The above table can be used to calculate the value of £1 at any time. For example, the RPI for June 1955 was 11.00 and for November 1988, 110.00. Thus £1 in June 1955 was worth £10 in November 1988.

Average Earnings Index

	1981	1982	1983	1984	1985	1986	1987	1988	1989	1990	1991
January	54.50	60.43	65.73	70.40	75.22	81.39	87.64	95.40	104.20	113.80	124.30
February	54.97	61.22	67.08	70.87	75.78	81.87	87.96	95.50	104.60	114.00	124.70
March	55.92	62.01	67.39	71.11	77.36	84.00	89.54	98.30	107.30	117.40	127.50
April	56.16	62.01	67.31	71.27	77.99	84.72	90.17	97.80	107.30	117.30	127.40
May	56.95	62.88	68.34	71.74	77.99	83.93	91.20	98.40	107.50	118.50	128.10
June	58.06	63.75	68.98	72.61	79.10	85.51	92.07	99.80	109.10	120.50	129.20
July	58.53	64.86	69.92	73.56	79.97	86.54	93.50	101.30	110.30	121.20	130.50
August	59.48	63.99	69.29	73.40	79.81	86.22	92.78	100.30	109.10	120.90	130.80
September	59.64	63.91	69.37	73.64	81.08	85.98	92.71	100.90	110.70	121.30	130.80
October	59.96	64.31	69.92	75.62	80.05	86.69	93.65	101.70	111.70	121.70	130.90
November	60.59	65.65	70.48	74.99	81.39	87.96	95.39	103.70	113.20	123.80	133.30
December	61.38	66.21	71.51	76.09	82.90	88.99	96.82	106.90	114.70	126.30	134.60

Average Weekly Earnings (£)

	Manufacturing industries		All industries and services	
	Including*	Excluding*	Including *	Excluding*
Males and females 18 years and over				
1981	116.8	122.5	119.8	123.1
1982 †	132.0	135.9	132.1	134.5
	131.2	135.2		
1983	141.2	146.0	143.2	146.1
Males and females on adult rates				
1983	142.2	147.0	144.5	147.4
1984	155.2	160.8	155.8	159.3
1985	169.2	174.7	167.4	171.0
1986	183.1	188.6	181.2	184.7
1987	196.0	202.0	194.9	198.9
1988	212.7	219.4	213.6	218.4
1989	231.7	239.5	234.3	239.7
1990	255.1	262.8	258.0	263.1
1991	271.3	280.7	278.9	284.7

* including/excluding those whose pay was affected by absence.

† Results for manufacturing industries in the first row of figures for 1982 relate to orders 3 to 19 inclusive of the 1968 Standard Industrial Classification ("SIC"). Results for manufacturing industries for 1983 to 1988 inclusive and the second row of figures for 1982 relate to divisions 2, 3 and 4 of the 1980 SIC.

House Price Index Statistics

(Reproduced with the kind permission of the Nationwide Anglia Building Society. Average price of all properties (house price/average earnings ratio)

				1954	1955
Q1				2,000 (3.44)	2,040 (3.22)
Q2				2,010 (3.40)	2,080 (3.21)
Q3				2,000 (3.32)	2,080 (3.18)
Q4				1,990 (3.24)	2,080 (3.11)

	1956	1957	1958	1959	1960
Q1	2,120 (3.10)	2,170 (3.05)	2,200 (2.93)	2,230 (2.88)	2,350 (2.83)
Q2	2,150 (3.08)	2,170 (3.01)	2,200 (2.93)	2,260 (2.88)	2,400 (2.84)
Q3	2,150 (3.06)	2,180 (2.95)	2,210 (2.91)	2,280 (2.86)	2,470 (2.89)
Q4	2,150 (3.04)	2,180 (2.91)	2,220 (2.90)	2,330 (2.87)	2,500 (2.88)

	1961	1962	1963	1964	1965
Q1	2,580 (2.92)	2,740 (3.00)	2,950 (3.16)	3,220 (3.18)	3,510 (3.24)
Q2	2,620 (2.92)	2,790 (3.03)	3,030 (3.15)	3,320 (3.22)	3,590 (3.26)
Q3	2,650 (2.94)	2,840 (3.07)	3,060 (3.13)	3,370 (3.21)	3,630 (3.24)
Q4	2,730 (3.01)	2,870 (3.10)	3,160 (3.19)	3,420 (3.21)	3,670 (3.20)

	1966	1967	1968	1969	1970
Q1	3,720 (3.19)	3,910 (3.26)	4,190 (3.25)	4,450 (3.21)	4,700 (3.08)
Q2	3,820 (3.21)	3,970 (3.27)	4,290 (3.28)	4,510 (3.19)	4,780 (3.03)
Q3	3,820 (3.19)	4,040 (3.26)	4,350 (3.25)	4,540 (3.15)	4,840 (3.00)
Q4	3,850 (3.22)	4,120 (3.26)	4,390 (3.21)	4,630 (3.13)	4,920 (2.96)

	1971	1972	1973		
Q1	5,090 (3.00)	6,450 (3.46)	8,850 (4.17)		
Q2	5,270 (3.05)	7,040 (3.66)	9,310 (4.21)		
Q3	5,630 (3.17)	7,940 (4.00)	9,680 (4.23)		
Q4	5,940 (3.29)	8,460 (4.07)	9,760 (4.11)		

	1974*	1975	1976	1977	1978
Q1*	10,465 (4.41)	10,950 (3.56)	12,142 (3.30)	13,081 (3.23)	14,568 (3.24)
Q2	10,570 (4.10)	11,309 (3.51)	12,374 (3.28)	13,376 (3.25)	15,275 (3.25)
Q3	10,697 (3.89)	11,572 (3.38)	12,648 (3.25)	13,672 (3.26)	16,773 (3.47)
Q4	10,760 (3.66)	11,899 (3.34)	12,870 (3.24)	13,862 (3.19)	17,733 (3.57)

	1979	1980	1981	1982	1983
Q1	18,756 (3.65)	23,904 (3.84)	25,014 (3.47)	25,485 (3.19)	27,731 (3.20)
Q2	20,107 (3.75)	24,611 (3.74)	25,402 (3.45)	26,014 (3.21)	28,868 (3.29)
Q3	21,594 (3.83)	24,907 (3.60)	25,497 (3.33)	26,320 (3.17)	29,700 (3.33)
Q4	23,155 (3.89)	24,769 (3.49)	25,086 (3.19)	26,964 (3.19)	30,172 (3.34)

	1984	1985	1986	1987	1988
Q1	31,281 (3.41)	34,997 (3.55)	37,576 (3.52)	43,094 (3.78)	47,531 (3.84)
Q2	32,501 (3.52)	36,023 (3.55)	39,018 (3.55)	45,313 (3.85)	51,580 (4.02)
Q3	32,945 (3.49)	36,578 (3.52)	40,321 (3.61)	46,838 (3.90)	57,293 (4.37)
Q4	34,304 (3.55)	37,354 (3.54)	41,736 (3.68)	46,755 (3.80)	60,343 (4.45)

	1989	1990	1991		
Q1	62,756 (4.56)	62,803 (4.18)	57,681 (3.48)		
Q2	65,605 (4.65)	62,150 (4.01)	58,707 (3.49)		
Q3	66,179 (4.61)	60,317 (3.82)	58,353 (3.42)		
Q4	64,823 (4.38)	57,869 (3.59)	56,889 (3.27†)		

* The figures for 1954 to 1973 are taken from an old set of tables that was eventually discontinued, whereas the figures for 1974 onwards are derived from the tables in current use. At the changeover point (Q1 in 1974) the figures in the old table were 9920 (4.18).
† estimated

FT - SE 100 Share index

(at start of each month)

	1984	1985	1986	1987	1988	1989	1990	1991	1992
January	1001.0	1230.3	1412.2	1677.6	1725.9	1783.2	2442.4	2142.9	2483.1
February	1062.6	1275.2	1431.5	1821.5	1797.3	2051.3	2346.5	2168.5	2563.7
March	1042.1	1256.7	1545.2	1986.6	1781.0	2017.2	2246.2	2374.9	2552.2
April	1115.5	1276.7	1671.3	1997.1	1734.4	2064.1	2224.3	2440.2	
May	1134.5	1293.7	1631.6	2064.4	1801.3	2114.8	2111.8	2487.4	
June	1026.8	1315.8	1604.4	2210.0	1779.6	2119.9	2345.3	2497.7	
July	1041.3	1229.9	1652.5	2272.6	1858.8	2154.9	2373.6	2416.7	
August	1009.5	1271.7	1555.0	2356.1	1861.1	2292.4	2329.3	2586.2	
September	1105.6	1335.1	1655.3	2261.6	1743.8	2392.1	2166.2	2653.9	
October	1137.5	1292.8	1561.0	2372.1	1811.4	2298.6	2006.3	2643.4	
November	1148.4	1372.1	1641.9	1717.5	1853.5	2146.0	2039.9	2559.0	
December	1187.9	1439.6	1637.8	1589.0	1785.3	2297.3	2159.7	2412.4	

FT 30 Share index

(at end of each year)

Year	Value	Year	Value	Year	Value	Year	Value	Year	Value
1950	115.7	1960	310.3	1970	340.6	1980	474.5	1990	1673.7
1951	121.9	1961	304.8	1971	476.5	1981	530.4	1991	1891.6
1952	115.8	1962	283.1	1972	505.4	1982	596.7		
1953	130.7	1963	348.3	1973	344.0	1983	775.7		
1954	184.0	1964	335.0	1974	161.4	1984	952.3		
1955	200.4	1965	339.7	1975	375.7	1985	1131.4		
1956	178.8	1966	310.3	1976	354.7	1986	1313.9		
1957	165.3	1967	389.2	1977	485.4	1987	1373.3		
1958	225.5	1968	506.4	1978	470.9	1988	1455.3		
1959	338.4	1969	407.4	1979	414.2	1989	1916.6		

Source material: *Financial Times*

Inheritance Tax

Rates

	17.3.87 - 14.3.88	15.3.88 - 5.4.89	6.4.89 - 5.4.90	6.4.90 - 5.4.91	6.4.91 - 5.4.92	10.3.92† -
Death rates/Full rates (%) *	0 - 60	0 & 40	0 & 40	0 & 40	0 & 40	0 & 40
Lifetime rates/Half rates (%)*	0 - 30	0 & 20	0 & 20	0 & 20	0 & 20	0 & 20
Maximum rates apply to cumulative chargeable transfers (gross) over - £	330,000	100,000	118,000	128,000	140,000	147,000
	1987/88	*1988/89*	*1989/90*	*1990/91*	*1991/92*	*1992/93*
Annual exemption **	£3,000	£3,000	£3,000	£3,000	£3,000	£3,000

* Detailed tables are set out on page 52.

† If Budget changes enacted, then £150,000 from 10.3.92

** Any unused exemption can be carried forward one year. The current exemption must be used first. Spouses are both entitled to annual exemptions. In previous years the exemptions were:

1973/74 to 1975/76	1976/77 to 1980/81	1981/82 to 1986/87
£1,000 p.a.	£2,000 p.a.	£3,000 p.a.

Reliefs and exemptions

The following is a checklist of the main reliefs and exemptions:

- *Agricultural property relief* - at 50% (from 10.3.92 100%) (where transferor has vacant possession or right to obtain it within a year); or 30%(from 10.3.92 50%) (pre-15.3.83, 20%) in other cases. Different conditions applied before 10.3.81.
- *Annual exemption* - see Table above.
- *Business property relief* - varies according to relevant business property:

	% from 10.3.92	%	
Business or interest in business	100	50	27.10.77 onwards *
Controlling shareholding (fully quoted)	50 (no change)	50	27.10.77 onwards *
Controlling shareholding (unquoted)	100 (incl USM cos)	50	27.10.77 onwards *
Substantial (over 25%) minority shareholding in unquoted company	100 (incl USM cos)	50	16.3.87 onwards *
Insubstantial (up to 25%) minority shareholding in unquoted company	50 (incl USM cos)	30	15.3.83 onwards *
Land, buildings, machinery or plant owned by certain individuals	50	30	6.4.76 onwards
Land, buildings, machinery or plant owned on certain trusts	50	30	9.3.81 onwards

  * A lower percentage applied before these dates
- *Charities* - transfers to charities exempt (pre-15.3.83 exempt up to a limit).
- *Employee trusts* - transfers by close companies and individuals to employee trusts can be exempt.
- *Marriage* - gifts in consideration of marriage are exempt up to limits varying according to donor:

Donor	Amount
Parent	£5,000
Grandparent or remoter ancestor	£2,500
Bride or groom	£2,500
Other	£1,000

- *Married couples* - transfers between spouses exempt unless the transferor (but not the other spouse) is UK domiciled when the limit is £55,000.
- *Normal expenditure out of income* - exempt.
- *Political parties* - transfers are exempt (unless made before 15.3.88 on or within one year of death when limited to £100,000).
- *Quick succession relief* - where death within first year, 100% relief; where within second to fifth year, decrease by 20% for each additional year survived.
- *Small gifts to any one person* - exempt if gift does not exceed £250 (before 6.4.81 the gift could exceed the exempt amount. Exemption was £100 to 5.4.80).
- *Tapering relief for inheritance tax* - applies at death in taxing transfers on or within 7 years of death. Current full rates, applied to values at time of lifetime transfers, are tapered as follows:

Years between transfer and death	% of full rates
0 - 3	100
3 - 4	80
4 - 5	60
5 - 6	40
6 - 7	20

- *Variations* - rearrangements of estates within 2 years of death.

Inheritance Tax Tables

Cumulative chargeable transfers (gross)	Band (gross) £	Rate on gross %	Tax on band (gross)	Cumulative tax	Cumulative chargeable transfers (net)	Rate on net
Full rates (death)						
6 April 1992 -						
(see opposite) 0 - 147,000	147,000	0	0	0	0 - 147,000	nil
147,000 +	-	40	-	-	147,000 +	2/3
6 April 1991 - 5 April 1992						
0 - 140,000	140,000	0	0	0	0 - 140,000	nil
140,000 +	-	40	-	-	140,000 +	2/3
6 April 1990 - 5 April 1991						
0 - 128,000	128,000	0	0	0	0 - 128,000	nil
128,000 +	-	40	-	-	128,000 +	2/3
6 April 1989 -5 April 1990						
0 - 118,000	118,000	0	0	0	0 - 118,000	nil
118,000 +	-	40	-	-	118,000 +	2/3
15 March 1988 - 5 April 1989						
0 - 110,000	110,000	0	0	0	0 - 110,000	nil
110,000 +	-	40	-	-	110,000 +	2/3
Half rates						
6 April 1992 -						
(see opposite) 0 - 147,000	147,000	0	0	0	- 147,000	nil
147,000 +	- 20		-	-	147,000 +	1/4
6 April 1991 - 5 April 1992						
0 - 140,000	140,000	0	0	0	0 - 140,000	nil
140,000 +	-	20	-	-	140,000 +	1/4
6 April 1990 - 5 April 1991						
0 - 128,000	128,000	0	0	0	0 - 128,000	nil
128,000 +	-	20	-	-	128,000 +	1/4
6 April 1989 -5 April 1990						
0 - 118,000	118,000	0	0	0	0 - 118,000	nil
118,000 +	-	20	-	-	118,000 +	1/4
15 March 1988 - 5 April 1989						
0 - 110,000	110,000	0	0	0	0 - 110,000	nil
110,000 +	-	20	-	-	110,000 +	1/4

Cumulative chargeable transfers (gross)	Band (gross) £	Rate on gross %	Tax on band (gross)	Cumulative tax	Cumulative chargeable transfers (net)	Rate on net
17 March 1987 - 14 March 1988						
Full rates (Death)						
0 - 90,000	90,000	0	0	0	0 - 90,000	nil
90,000 - 140,000	50,000	30	15,000	15,000	90,000 - 125,000	3/7
140,000 - 220,000	80,000	40	32,000	47,000	125,000 - 173,000	2/3
220,000 - 330,000	110,000	50	55,000	102,000	173,000 - 228,000	1
330,000 +	-	60	-	-	228,000 +	1 1/2
Half rates						
0 - 90,000	90,000	0	0	0	0 - 90,000	nil
90,000 - 140,000	50,000	15	7,500	7,500	90,000 - 132,500	3/17
140,000 - 220,000	80,000	20	16,000	23,500	132,500 - 196,500	1/4
220,000 - 330,000	110,000	25	27,500	51,000	196,500 - 279,000	1/3
330,000 +	-	30	-	-	279,000 +	3/7
18 March 1986 - 16 March 1987						
Full rates (Death)						
0 - 71,000	71,000	0	0	0	0 - 71,000	nil
71,000 - 95,000	24,000	30	7,200	7,200	71,000 - 87,800	3/7
95,000 - 129,000	34,000	35	11,900	19,100	87,800 - 109,900	7/13
129,000 - 164,000	35,000	40	14,000	33,100	109,900 - 130,900	2/3
164,000 - 206,000	42,000	45	18,900	52,000	130,900 - 154,000	9/11
206,000 - 257,000	51,000	50	25,500	77,500	154,000 - 179,500	1
257,000 - 317,000	60,000	55	33,000	110,500	179,500 - 206,500	1 2/9
317,000 +	-	60	-	-	206,500 +	1 1/2
Half rates						
0 - 71,000	71,000	0	0	0	0 - 71,000	nil
71,000 - 95,000	24,000	15	3,600	3,600	71,000 - 91,400	3/17
95,000 - 129,000	34,000	17.5	5,950	9,550	91,400 - 119,450	7/33
129,000 - 164,000	35,000	20	7,000	16,550	119,450 - 147,450	1/4
164,000 - 206,000	42,000	22.5	9,450	26,000	147,450 - 180,000	9/31
206,000 - 257,000	51,000	25	12,750	38,750	180,000 - 218,250	1/3
257,000 - 317,000	60,000	27.5	16,500	55,250	218,250 - 261,750	11/29
317,000 +	-	30	-	-	261,750 +	3/7

Capital Transfer Tax Tables

Cumulative chargeable transfers (gross)	Band (gross) £	Rate on gross%	Tax on band (gross)	Cumulative tax	Cumulative chargeable transfers (net)	Rate on net
6 April 1985 - 17 March 1986						
Death rates						
0 - 67,000	67,000	0	nil	nil	0 - 67,000	nil
67,000 - 89,000	22,000	30	6,600	6,600	67,000 - 82,400	3/7
89,000 - 122,000	33,000	35	11,550	18,150	82,400 - 103,850	7/13
122,000 - 155,000	33,000	40	13,200	31,350	103,850 - 123,650	2/3
155,000 - 194,000	39,000	45	17,550	48,900	123,650 - 145,100	9/11
194,000 - 243,000	49,000	50	24,500	73,400	145,100 - 169,600	1
243,000 - 299,000	56,000	55	30,800	104,200	169,600 - 194,800	1 2/9
299,000 +	-	60	-	-	194,800 +	1 1/2
Lifetime rates						
0 - 67,000	67,000	0	nil	nil	0 - 67,000	nil
67,000 - 89,000	22,000	15	3,300	3,300	67,000 - 85,700	3/17
89,000 - 122,000	33,000	17.5	5,775	9,075	85,700 - 112,925	7/33
122,000 - 155,000	33,000	20	6,600	15,675	112,925 - 139,325	1/4
155,000 - 194,000	39,000	22.5	8,775	24,450	139,325 - 169,550	9/31
194,000 - 243,000	49,000	25	12,250	36,700	169,550 - 206,300	1/3
243,000 - 299,000	56,000	27.5	15,400	52,100	206,300 - 246,900	11/29
299,000 +	-	30	-	-	246,900 +	3/7
13 March 1984 - 5 April 1985						
Death rates						
0 - 64,000	64,000	0	nil	nil	0 - 64,000	nil
64,000 - 85,000	21,000	30	6,300	6,300	64,000 - 78,700	3/7
85,000 - 116,000	31,000	35	10,850	17,150	78,700 - 98,850	7/13
116,000 - 148,000	32,000	40	12,800	29,950	98,850 - 118,050	2/3
148,000 - 185,000	37,000	45	16,650	46,600	118,050 - 138,400	9/11
185,000 - 232,000	47,000	50	23,500	70,100	138,400 - 161,900	1
232,000 - 285,000	53,000	55	29,150	99,250	161,900 - 185,750	1 2/9
285,000 +	-	60	-	-	185,750 +	1 1/2
Lifetime rates						
0 - 64,000	64,000	0	nil	nil	0 - 64,000	nil
64,000 - 85,000	21,000	15	3,150	3,150	64,000 - 81,850	3/17
85,000 - 116,000	31,000	17.5	5,425	8,575	81,850 - 107,425	7/33
116,000 - 148,000	32,000	20	6,400	14,975	107,425 - 133,025	1/4
148,000 - 185,000	37,000	22.5	8,325	23,300	133,025 - 161,700	9/31
185,000 - 232,000	47,000	25	11,750	35,050	161,700 - 196,950	1/3
232,000 - 285,000	53,000	27.5	14,575	49,625	196,950 - 235,375	11/29
285,000 +	-	30	-	-	235,375 +	3/7
15 March 1983 - 12 March 1984						
Death rates						
0 - 60,000	60,000	0	nil	nil	0 - 60,000	nil
60,000 - 80,000	20,000	30	6,000	6,000	60,000 - 74,000	3/7
80,000 - 110,000	30,000	35	10,500	16,500	74,000 - 93,500	7/13
110,000 - 140,000	30,000	40	12,000	28,500	93,500 - 111,500	2/3
140,000 - 175,000	35,000	45	15,750	44,250	111,500 - 130,750	9/11
175,000 - 220,000	45,000	50	22,500	66,750	130,750 - 153,250	1
220,000 - 270,000	50,000	55	27,500	94,250	153,250 - 175,750	1 2/9
270,000 - 700,000	430,000	60	258,000	352,250	175,750 - 347,750	1 1/2
700,000 - 1,325,000	625,000	65	406,250	758,500	347,750 - 566,500	1 6/7
1,325,000 - 2,650,000	1,325,000	70	927,500	1,686,000	566,500 - 964,000	2 1/3
2,650,000 +	-	75	-	-	964,000 +	3

Cumulative chargeable transfers (gross)	Band (gross) £	Rate on gross%	Tax on band (gross)	Cumulative tax	Cumulative chargeable transfers (net)	Rate on net
Lifetime rates						
0- 60,000	60,000	0	nil	nil	0 - 60,000	nil
60,000 - 80,000	20,000	15	3,000	3,000	60,000 - 77,000	3/17
80,000 -110,000	30,000	17.5	5,250	8,250	77,000 - 101,750	7/33
110,000 -140,000	30,000	20	6,000	14,250	101,750 - 125,750	1/4
140,000 -175,000	35,000	22.5	7,875	22,125	125,750 - 152,875	9/31
175,000 -220,000	45,000	25	11,250	33,375	152,875 - 186,625	1/3
220,000 -270,000	50,000	30	15,000	48,375	186,625 - 221,625	3/7
270,000 -700,000	430,000	35	150,500	198,875	221,625 - 501,125	7/13
700,000 -1,325,000	625,000	40	250,000	448,875	501,125 - 876,125	2/3
1,325,000 -2,650,000	1,325,000	45	596,250	1,045,125	876,125 -1,604,875	9/11
2,650,000 +	-	50	-	-	1,604,875 +	1
9 March 1982 - 14 March 1983						
Death rates						
0 - 55,000	55,000	0	nil	nil	0 - 55,000	nil
55,000 - 75,000	20,000	30	6,000	6,000	55,000 - 69,000	3/7
75,000 -100,000	25,000	35	8,750	14,750	69,000 - 85,250	7/13
100,000 -130,000	30,000	40	12,000	26,750	85,250- 103,250	2/3
130,000 -165,000	35,000	45	15,750	42,500	103,250 - 122,500	9/11
165,000 -200,000	35,000	50	17,500	60,000	122,500 - 140,000	1
200,000 -250,000	50,000	55	27,500	87,500	140,000 - 162,500	1 2/9
250,000 -650,000	400,000	60	240,000	327,500	162,500 - 322,500	1 1/2
650,000 -1,250,000	600,000	65	390,000	717,500	322,500 - 532,500	1 6/7
1,250,000 -2,500,000	1,250,000	70	875,000	1,592,500	532,500 - 907,500	2 1/3
2,500,000 +	-	75	-	-	907,500 +	3
Lifetime rates						
0 - 55,000	55,000	0	nil	nil	0 - 55,000	nil
55,000 - 75,000	20,000	15	3,000	3,000	55,000 - 72,000	3/17
75,000 -100,000	25,000	17.5	4,375	7,375	72,000 - 92,625	7/33
100,000 -130,000	30,000	20	6,000	13,375	92,625 - 116,625	1/4
130,000 -165,000	35,000	22.5	7,875	21,250	116,625 - 143,750	9/31
165,000 -200,000	35,000	25	8,750	30,000	143,750 - 170,000	1/3
200,000 -250,000	50,000	30	15,000	45,000	170,000 - 205,000	3/7
250,000 -650,000	400,000	35	140,000	185,000	205,000 - 465,000	7/13
650,000 -1,250,000	600,000	40	240,000	425,000	465,000 - 825,000	2/3
1,250,000 -2,500,000	1,250,000	45	562,500	987,500	825,000 -1,512,500	9/11
2,500,000 +	-	50	-	-	1,512,500 +	1
10 March 1981 to 8 March 1982						
Death rates						
0 - 50,000	50,000	0	nil	nil	0 - 50,000	nil
50,000 - 60,000	10,000	30	3,000	3,000	50,000 - 57,000	3/7
60,000 - 70,000	10,000	35	3,500	6,500	57,000 - 63,500	7/13
70,000 - 90,000	20,000	40	8,000	14,500	63,500 - 75,500	2/3
90,000 -110,000	20,000	45	9,000	23,500	75,500 - 86,500	9/11
110,000 -130,000	20,000	50	10,000	33,500	86,500 - 96,500	1
130,000 -160,000	30,000	55	16,500	50,000	96,500 - 110,000	1 2/9
160,000 -510,000	350,000	60	210,000	260,000	110,000 - 250,000	1 1/2
510,000 -1,010,000	500,000	65	325,000	585,000	250,000 - 425,000	1 6/7
1,010,000 -2,010,000	1,000,000	70	700,000	1,285,000	425,000 - 725,000	2 1/3
2,010,000 +	-	75	-	-	725,000 +	3
Lifetime rates						
0 - 50,000	50,000	0	nil	nil	0 - 50,000	nil
50,000 - 60,000	10,000	15	1,500	1,500	50,000 - 58,500	3/17
60,000 - 70,000	10,000	17.5	1,750	3,250	58,500 - 66,750	7/33
70,000 - 90,000	20,000	20	4,000	7,250	66,750 - 82,750	1/4
90,000 -110,000	20,000	22.5	4,500	11,750	82,750 - 98,250	9/31
110,000 -130,000	20,000	25	5,000	16,750	98,250 - 113,250	1/3
130,000 -160,000	30,000	30	9,000	25,750	113,250 - 134,250	3/7
160,000 -510,000	350,000	35	122,500	148,250	134,250 - 361,750	7/13
510,000 -1,010,000	500,000	40	200,000	348,250	361,750 - 661,750	2/3
1,010,000 -2,010,000	1,000,000	45	450,000	798,250	661,750 -1,211,750	9/11
2,010,000 +	-	50	-	-	1,211,750 +	1

Cumulative chargeable transfers (gross)	Band (gross) £	Rate on gross%	Tax on band (gross)	Cumulative tax	Cumulative chargeable transfers (net)	Rate on net
26 March 1980 to 9 March 1981						
Death rates						
0 - 50,000	50,000	0	nil	nil	0 - 50,000	nil
50,000 - 60,000	10,000	30	3,000	3,000	50,000 - 57,000	$\frac{3}{7}$
60,000 - 70,000	10,000	35	3,500	6,500	57,000 - 63,500	$\frac{7}{13}$
70,000 - 90,000	20,000	40	8,000	14,500	63,500 - 75,500	$\frac{2}{3}$
90,000 - 110,000	20,000	45	9,000	23,500	75,500 - 86,500	$\frac{9}{11}$
110,000 - 130,000	20,000	50	10,000	33,500	86,500 - 96,500	1
130,000 - 160,000	30,000	55	16,500	50,000	96,500 - 110,000	$1\frac{2}{9}$
160,000 - 510,000	350,000	60	210,000	260,000	110,000 - 250,000	$1\frac{1}{2}$
510,000 - 1,010,000	500,000	65	325,000	585,000	250,000 - 425,000	$1\frac{6}{7}$
1,010,000 - 2,010,000	1,000,000	70	700,000	1,285,000	425,000 - 725,000	$2\frac{1}{3}$
2,010,000 +	-	75	-	-	725,000 +	3
Lifetime rates						
0 - 50,000	50,000	0	nil	nil	0 - 50,000	nil
50,000 - 60,000	10,000	15	1,500	1,500	50,000 - 58,500	$\frac{3}{17}$
60,000 - 70,000	10,000	17.5	1,750	3,250	58,500 - 66,750	$\frac{7}{33}$
70,000 - 90,000	20,000	20	4,000	7,250	66,750 - 82,750	$\frac{1}{4}$
90,000 - 110,000	20,000	22.5	4,500	11,750	82,750 - 98,250	$\frac{9}{31}$
110,000 - 130,000	20,000	27.5	5,500	17,250	98,250 - 112,750	$\frac{11}{29}$
130,000 - 160,000	30,000	35	10,500	27,750	112,750 - 132,250	$\frac{7}{13}$
160,000 - 210,000	50,000	42.5	21,250	49,000	132,250 - 161,000	$\frac{17}{23}$
210,000 - 260,000	50,000	50	25,000	74,000	161,000 - 186,000	1
260,000 - 310,000	50,000	55	27,500	101,500	186,000 - 208,500	$1\frac{2}{9}$
310,000 - 510,000	200,000	60	120,000	221,500	208,500 - 288,500	$1\frac{1}{2}$
510,000 - 1,010,000	500,000	65	325,000	546,500	288,500 - 463,500	$1\frac{6}{7}$
1,010,000 - 2,010,000	1,000,000	70	700,000	1,246,500	463,500 - 763,500	$2\frac{1}{3}$
2,010,000 +	-	75	-	-	763,500 +	3
27 October 1977 - 25 March 1980						
Death rates						
0 - 25,000	25,000	0	nil	nil	0 - 25,000	nil
25,000 - 30,000	5,000	10	500	500	25,000 - 29,500	$\frac{1}{9}$
30,000 - 35,000	5,000	15	750	1,250	29,500 - 33,750	$\frac{3}{17}$
35,000 - 40,000	5,000	20	1,000	2,250	33,750 - 37,750	$\frac{1}{4}$
40,000 - 50,000	10,000	25	2,500	4,750	37,750 - 45,250	$\frac{1}{3}$
50,000 - 60,000	10,000	30	3,000	7,750	45,250 - 52,250	$\frac{3}{7}$
60,000 - 70,000	10,000	35	3,500	11,250	52,250 - 58,750	$\frac{7}{13}$
70,000 - 90,000	20,000	40	8,000	19,250	58,750 - 70,750	$\frac{2}{3}$
90,000 - 110,000	20,000	45	9,000	28,250	70,750 - 81,750	$\frac{9}{11}$
110,000 - 130,000	20,000	50	10,000	38,250	81,750 - 91,750	1
130,000 - 160,000	30,000	55	16,500	54,750	91,750 - 105,250	$1\frac{2}{9}$
160,000 - 510,000	350,000	60	210,000	264,750	105,250 - 245,250	$1\frac{1}{2}$
510,000 - 1,010,000	500,000	65	325,000	589,750	245,250 - 420,250	$1\frac{6}{7}$
1,010,000 - 2,010,000	1,000,000	70	700,000	1,289,750	420,250 - 720,250	$2\frac{1}{3}$
2,010,000 +	-	75	-	-	720,250 +	3
Lifetime rates						
0 - 25,000	25,000	0	nil	nil	0 - 25,000	nil
25,000 - 30,000	5,000	5	250	250	25,000 - 29,750	$\frac{1}{19}$
30,000 - 35,000	5,000	7.5	375	625	29,750 - 34,375	$\frac{3}{37}$
35,000 - 40,000	5,000	10	500	1,125	34,375 - 38,875	$\frac{1}{9}$
40,000 - 50,000	10,000	12.5	1,250	2,375	38,875 - 47,625	$\frac{1}{7}$
50,000 - 60,000	10,000	15	1,500	3,875	47,625 - 56,125	$\frac{3}{17}$
60,000 - 70,000	10,000	17.5	1,750	5,625	56,125 - 64,375	$\frac{7}{33}$
70,000 - 90,000	20,000	20	4,000	9,625	64,375 - 80,375	$\frac{1}{4}$
90,000 - 110,000	20,000	22.5	4,500	14,125	80,375 - 95,875	$\frac{9}{31}$
110,000 - 130,000	20,000	27.5	5,500	19,625	95,875 - 110,375	$\frac{11}{29}$
130,000 - 160,000	30,000	35	10,500	30,125	110,375 - 129,875	$\frac{7}{13}$
160,000 - 210,000	50,000	42.5	21,250	51,375	129,875 - 158,625	$\frac{17}{23}$
210,000 - 260,000	50,000	50	25,000	76,375	158,625 - 183,625	1
260,000 - 310,000	50,000	55	27,500	103,875	183,625 - 206,125	$1\frac{2}{9}$
310,000 - 510,000	200,000	60	120,000	223,875	206,125 - 286,125	$1\frac{1}{2}$
510,000 - 1,010,000	500,000	65	325,000	548,875	286,125 - 461,125	$1\frac{6}{7}$
1,010,000 - 2,010,000	1,000,000	70	700,000	1,248,875	461,125 - 761,125	$2\frac{1}{3}$
2,010,000 +	-	75	-	-	761,125 +	3

Cumulative chargeable transfers (gross)	Band (gross) £	Rate on gross%	Tax on band (gross)	Cumulative tax	Cumulative chargeable transfers (net)	Rate on net
Before 27 October 1977						
Death rates						
0 - 15,000	15,000	0	nil	nil	0 - 15,000	nil
15,000 - 20,000	5,000	10	500	500	15,000 - 19,500	1/9
20,000 - 25,000	5,000	15	750	1,250	19,500 - 23,750	3/17
25,000 - 30,000	5,000	20	1,000	2,250	23,750 - 27,750	1/4
30,000 - 40,000	10,000	25	2,500	4,750	27,750 - 35,250	1/3
40,000 - 50,000	10,000	30	3,000	7,750	35,250 - 42,250	3/7
50,000 - 60,000	10,000	35	3,500	11,250	42,250 - 48,750	7/13
60,000 - 80,000	20,000	40	8,000	19,250	48,750 - 60,750	2/3
80,000 -100,000	20,000	45	9,000	28,250	60,750 - 71,750	9/11
100,000 -120,000	20,000	50	10,000	38,250	71,750 - 81,750	1
120,000 -150,000	30,000	55	16,500	54,750	81,750 - 95,250	1 2/9
150,000 -500,000	350,000	60	210,000	264,750	95,250 - 235,250	1 1/2
500,000 -1,000,000	500,000	65	325,000	589,750	235,250 - 410,250	1 6/7
1,000,000 -2,000,000	1,000,000	70	700,000	1,289,750	410,250 - 710,250	2 1/3
2,000,000 +		75			710,250 +	3
Lifetime rates						
0 - 15,000	15,000	0	nil	nil	0 - 15,000	nil
15,000 - 20,000	5,000	5	250	250	15,000 - 19,750	1/19
20,000 - 25,000	5,000	7.5	375	625	19,750 - 24,375	3/37
25,000 - 30,000	5,000	10	500	1,125	24,375 - 28,875	1/9
30,000 - 40,000	10,000	12.5	1,250	2,375	28,875 - 37,625	1/7
40,000 - 50,000	10,000	15	1,500	3,875	37,625 - 46,125	3/17
50,000 - 60,000	10,000	17.5	1,750	5,625	46,125 - 54,375	7/33
60,000 - 80,000	20,000	20	4,000	9,625	54,375 - 70,375	1/4
80,000 -100,000	20,000	22.5	4,500	14,125	70,375 - 85,875	9/31
100,000 -120,000	20,000	27.5	5,500	19,625	85,875 - 100,375	11/29
120,000 -150,000	30,000	35	10,500	30,125	100,375 - 119,875	7/13
150,000 -200,000	50,000	42.5	21,250	51,375	119,875 - 148,625	17/23
200,000 -250,000	50,000	50	25,000	76,375	148,625 - 173,625	1
250,000 -300,000	50,000	55	27,500	103,875	173,625 - 196,125	1 2/9
300,000 -500,000	200,000	60	120,000	223,875	196,125 - 276,125	1 1/2
500,000 -1,000,000	500,000	65	325,000	548,875	276,125 - 451,125	1 6/7
1,000,000 -2,000,000	1,000,000	70	700,000	1,248,875	451,125 - 751,125	2 1/3
2,000,000 +		75			751,125 +	3

National Insurance Benefits
BENEFITS TAXABLE UNDER SCHEDULE E
Dates are unless otherwise stated; amounts are £ per week

	6.4.87 to 10.4.88	11.4.88 to 9.4.89	10.4.89 to 8.4.90	9.4.90 to 7.4.91	8.4.91 to 5.4.92	Total 1991/92 (52 new)	6.4.92 to 5.4.93	Total 1992/93 (52 new) [4]
Retirement pensions (basic)[1]								
Married couple:								
both contributors - each	39.50	41.15	43.60	46.90	52.00	2,704.00	54.15	2,815.80
wife non-contributor - addition	23.75	24.75	26.20	28.20	31.25	1,625.00	32.55	1,692.60
wife non-contributor - joint	63.25	65.90	69.80	75.10	83.25	4,329.00	86.10	4,508.40
Single person	39.50	41.15	43.60	46.90	52.00	2,704.00	54.15	2,815.80
Age addition (over 80): 25p per week (£13.00 p.a.)								
Non-contributory retirement pension [1]								
Married couple:								
Category C	37.95	39.55	41.85	45.05	49.95	2,597.40	52.00	2,704.00
Category D	47.50	49.50	52.40	56.40	62.50	3,250.00	65.10	3,385.20
Single person	23.75	24.75	26.20	28.20	31.25	1,625.00	32.55	1,692.60
Age addition (over 80): 25p per week (£13.00 p.a.)								
Industrial death benefit [2]								
Widow's pension (first 26 weeks)	55.35	57.65	-	-				
Higher permanent rate	40.05	41.15	43.60	46.90	52.00	2,704.00	54.15	2,815.80
Lower permanent rate	11.85	12.35	13.08	14.07	15.60	811.20	16.25	845.00
Widow's benefits								
Widow's allowance (1st 26 wks)	55.35	57.65	43.60[3]	46.90[3]	52.00[3]	2,704.00	54.15[3]	2,815.80
Widow's pension (after first 26 wks standard rate)	39.50	41.15	43.60	46.90	52.00	2,704.00	54.15	2,815.80
Widowed mother's allowance	39.50	41.15	43.60	46.90	52.00	2,704.00	54.15	2,815.80
Invalidity allowance (when paid with retirement pension)								
Higher rate	8.30	8.65	9.20	10.00	11.10	577.20	11.55	600.60
Middle rate	5.30	5.50	5.80	6.20	6.90	358.80	7.20	374.40
Lower rate	2.65	2.75	2.90	3.10	3.45	179.40	3.60	187.20
Invalid care allowance								
Each individual	23.75	24.75	26.20	28.20	31.25	1,625.00	32.55	1,692.60
Increase for adult dependant	14.20	14.80	15.65	16.85	18.70	972.40	19.45	1,011.40
Unemployment benefit								
Single person	31.45	32.75	34.70	37.35	41.40	2,152.80	43.10	2,241.20
Increase for adult dependant	19.40	20.20	21.40	23.05	25.55	1,328.60	26.60	1,383.20

[1] See earnings rule, opposite

[2] Industrial death benefit is payable in respect of deaths before 11 April 1988 only.

[3] Plus a tax-free lump sum widow's payment of £1,000. Widow's allowance has been abolished and widow's pension is now payable both during the first 26 weeks and thereafter. These changes apply to new claims from 11 April 1988.

[4] In some cases, a saving may be achieved by calculating 1 week at the old rate and 51 at the new rate.

Retirement Pension: Earnings Rules

Applying for first five years over pensionable age

	25.11.85 - 30.9.89
Earnings limit (per week)	£75
Pension reduced by 5p:	
(i) for each complete 10p above limit up to	£79
(ii) and for each complete 5p earned over	

The retirement pension earnings rules were abolished from 1 October 1989.

Job Release Allowances

(Taxable except for men aged 64 and women aged 59. The Job Release Scheme finished on 31 January 1988 except for those already receiving payments then.)

	6.4.87 to 10.4.88	11.4.88 to 9.4.89	10.4.89 to 8.4.90	9.4.90 to 7.4.91	8.4.91 to 5.4.92	6.4.92 to 5.4.93
Married man (with dependent wife earning less than £17* per week)	74.50	75.50	79.25	84.00	90.70	94.45
Other persons	61.15	62.15	65.25	69.15	74.70	77.80

* £15 per week up to 7.4.91, then £16 per week to 5.4.92

Statutory Pay
Statutory sick pay

Year	Average weekly earnings	Weekly rate
6.4.92 - 5.4.93	Under £54.00	nil
	£54.00 - £189.99	£45.30
	Over £190.00	£52.50
6.4.91 - 5.4.92	Under £52.00	nil
	£52.00 - £184.99	£43.50
	Over £185.00	£52.50
6.4.90 - 5.4.91	Under £46.00	nil
	£46.00 - £124.99	£39.25
	Over £125.00	£52.50
6.4.89 - 5.4.90	Under £43.00	nil
	£43.00 - £83.99	£36.25
	Over £84.00	£52.10
6.4.88 - 5.4.89	Under £41.00	nil
	£41.00 - £79.49	£34.25
	Over £79.50	£49.20
6.4.87 - 5.4.88	Under £39.00	nil
	£39.00 - £76.49	£32.85
	Over £76.50	£47.20

Statutory maternity pay

Year	Higher weekly rate	Lower weekly rate
6.4.92 - 5.4.93	90% of employee's normal weekly earnings	£46.30
6.4.91 - 5.4.92	90% of employee's normal weekly earnings	£44.50
6.4.90 - 5.4.91	90% of employee's normal weekly earnings	£39.25
6.4.89 - 5.4.90	90% of employee's normal weekly earnings	£36.25
6.4.88 - 5.4.89	90% of employee's normal weekly earnings	£34.25
6.4.87 - 5.4.88	90% of employee's normal weekly earnings	£32.88

National Insurance Benefits
NON-TAXABLE BENEFITS

Dates are unless otherwise stated; amounts are £ per week

	6.4.87 to 10.4.88	11.4.88 to 9.4.89	10.4.89 to 8.4.90	9.4.90 to 7.4.91	8.4.91 to 5.4.92	Total 1991/92 (52 new)	6.4.92 to 5.4.93	Total 1992/93 (52 new)
Child dependency additions When paid with invalid care allowance; retirement pension; widow's allowance or pension; or widowed mother's allowance	8.05	8.40	8.95	9.65	10.70	556.40	10.85	564.20
Child benefit	7.25	7.25	7.25	7.25	7.50†	390.00	7.80†	405.60
One parent benefit	4.70	4.90	5.20	5.60	5.60	291.20	5.85	304.20
Attendance Allowance[1]								
• higher rate	31.60	32.95	34.90	37.55	41.65	2,165.80	43.35[2]	2,254.20
• lower rate	20.65	21.10	22.00	25.05	27.80	1,445.60	28.95[2]	1,505.40
Industrial disablement benefit								
100%	64.50	67.20	71.20	76.60	84.90	4,414.80	88.40	4,596.80
Unemployability supplement	39.50	41.15	43.60	46.90	52.00	2,704.00	54.15	2,815.80
Constant attendance allowance (Normal maximum)	25.80	26.90	28.50	30.70	34.00	1,768.00	35.40	1,840.80
Exceptionally severe disablement allowance	25.80	26.90	28.50	30.70	34.00	1,768.00	35.40	1,840.80
Reduced earnings (special hardship) allowance	25.80	26.88	28.48	30.64	33.96	1,765.92	35.36	1,838.72
Invalidity benefit								
Personal benefit	39.50	41.15	43.60	46.90	52.00	2,704.00	54.15	2,815.80
Increase for adult dependant	23.75	24.75	26.20	28.20	31.25	1,625.00		
Increase for each child dependant	8.05	8.40	8.95	9.65	10.70	556.40		
Maternity allowance (standard personal benefit)	30.05	31.30	33.20	35.70	40.60	-	42.25	-
Mobility allowance[3]	22.10	23.05	24.40	26.25	29.10	1,513.20	30.30[4]	1,575.60
Sickness benefit								
Standard rate	30.05	31.30	33.20	35.70	39.60	2,059.20	41.20	2,142.40
Increase for dependent adult	18.60	19.40	20.55	22.10	24.50	1,274.00	25.50	1,326.00
Income support (tax free except to those required to register as unemployed)								
Married or unmarried couple	49.35	51.45*	54.80*	57.60*	62.25*	-	66.60*	-
Single householder	30.40	33.40**	34.90**	36.70**	39.65**	-	42.45**	-

* Payable where at least one is aged 18 or over
** Payable to single person aged 25 or over
† But £9.65 for the only, elder or eldest child for whom child benefit is payable.
1 Replaced (from April 1992) for those under 65 by Disability Living Allowance (DLA)
2 The rates quoted are the higher and middle rates of the care compenent of the DLA. The lower rate is £11.55.

3 Replaced from April 1992 by Disability Living Allowance
4 The rate quoted is the higher rate of the mobility component of the DLA. The lower rate is £11.55

Department of Social Security Leaflets

The list below gives the reference numbers and subjects of a selection of explanatory leaflets concerning social security which are published by the Department of Social Security to assist claimants, contributors and employers, and to give information in answer to enquiries. Except where otherwise stated, the leaflets are available at local offices of the Department (for individual copies), or by postal application only from DSS Leaflets Unit, PO Box 21, Stanmore, Middx HA7 1AY.

National Insurance (contributory) benefits
NI 1	National Insurance choices for married women
NI 24	National Insurance guide for Mariners
NI 27A	NI People with small earnings from self-employment
NI 35	NI for company directors
NI 38	Social Security abroad
NI 42	NI voluntary contributions
NI 47	NI guidance for share fishermen
NI 48	National Insurance: unpaid and late paid contributions
NI 51	National Insurance for widows
NI 95	NI guide for divorced women
NI 125	Training for further employment and your NI Record
NI 132	NI guide for employers of people working abroad
NI 192	NI for agencies and people employed through agencies
NI 222	NI for examiners and part-time lecturers, teachers and instructors
NI 244	Statutory Sick Pay - check your rights
NI 255	Class 2 and Class 3 National Insurance contributions. Direct Debit - The easy way to pay
NP 16	NI contributions for people working for embassies, consulates, or overseas employers
NP 18	Class 2 and Class 4 National Insurance Contributions
NP 28	National insurance for employees
NP 40	New pension choices

Employer's National Insurance
NI 25	NI guide for masters and employers of mariners
NI 132	NI for employers of people working abroad
NI 257	Employers guide to statutory maternity pay
NI 268	Quick guide to N.I., S.S.P. and S.M.P contributions
NI 269	Employer's manual on NI contributions
NI 270	Employer's manual on statutory sick pay
NP 23	Employer's guide: occupational pension schemes and contracting out
NP 29	Employer's guide to procedures on termination of contracted-out employment (from COE Group, DSS, Newcastle upon Tyne only)

Industrial Injury, Disease and Notes
NI 2	If you have an industrial disease
NI 3	Pneumoconiosis and Byssinosis
NI 6	Industrial injuries disablement benefit
NI 207	Occupational deafness
NI 237	Occupational asthma

National Insurance Benefits
NI 12	Unemployment Benefit
NI 14	Guardian's allowance
NI 16	Sickness Benefit
NI 16A	Invalidity benefit
NI 17A	Maternity benefits
NI 230	Unemployment benefit and your occupational or personal pension
NP 46	A guide to retirement pensions

Means Tested Benefits
RR 1   Housing Benefit – help with your rent
FC 1   Family Credit
SB 16   A Guide to the Social Fund
IS 1   Income Support
IS 20   A guide to Income Support

Non-Contributory Benefit
CH 1   Child Benefit
CH 11   One parent benefit
NI 184   Retirement pension for people over 80
DS 2   Attendance Allowance
NI 211   Mobility allowance
DS 700 Invalid care allowance
NI 252   Severe disablement allowance

Technical guides
D 49   What to do after a death
NI 261   Family credit
NP 45   Widows benefits
RR 2   Housing benefit and community charge benefit
HB 5   Non-contributory benefits for disabled people
NI 260   A guide to reviews and appeals

War Pensions
(These leaflets can be obtained from War Pensions Offices of the Department of Social Security.)
MPL 120 War Pensioners and war widows going abroad
MPL 152 War Widows and other dependants
MPL 153 Guide for war disabled
MPL 154 Rates of war pensions and allowance

Reciprocal agreements with other countries
(These leaflets are only available from Overseas Branch, DSS, Newcastle upon Tyne.)
SA 29   Your social security, health care and pension rights in the EC
SA 5   Australia
SA 25   Austria
SA 23   Bermuda
SA 20   Canada
SA 12   Cyprus
SA 19   Finland
SA 24   Iceland
SA 14   Israel
SA 27   Jamaica
SA 4   Jersey & Guernsey
SA 11   Malta
SA 38   Mauritius
SA 8   New Zealand
SA 16   Norway
SA 42   The Philippines
SA 9   Sweden
SA 6   Switzerland
SA 22   Turkey
SA 33   USA
SA 17   Yugoslavia

National Insurance Contributions
1992/93

Income limits

	Weekly	Monthly	Yearly
Lower earnings limit	£54.00	£234.00	£2,808
Upper earnings limit	£405.00	£1,755.00	£21,060

Class 1 Contributions
Standard rate (applying to all earnings)

Weekly earnings	Not contracted out		Contracted out			
	Employee	Employer	Employee On 1st £54	Remainder	Employer On 1st £54	Remainder
£54.00 - £89.99	9%*	4.6%	2%	7%	4.6%	0.8%
£90.00 - £134.99	9%*	6.6%	2%	7%	6.6%	2.8%
£135.00 - £189.99	9%*	8.6%	2%	7%	8.6%	4.8%
£190.00 - £405.00	9%*	10.4%	2%	7%	10.4%	6.6% up to £405
Over £405.00	9%*	10.4%	2%	7%	10.4%	10.4% over £405
* but with a rate of only 2% on the first £54 of earnings	on £405	on all earnings	up to overall limit £405		on all earnings	

Reduced rates

		Employee	Employer
Married women and widows with valid certificate of election:		3.85%	As in above columns
Men over 65 and women over 60		nil	As in not contracted out column
Children under 16		nil	nil

Class 2 Contributions

Self-employed persons	£5.35 per week
Share fishermen's rate	£7.00 per week
Small earnings exemption	£3,030 per year

None payable by men over 65 or women over 60

Class 3 Contributions

Voluntary contributions	£5.25 per week

Not payable if pensionable age reached during year of assessment

Class 4 Contributions

Self-employed (added to Class 2)	6.3% on profits or gains between £6,120 and £21,060 per year
Maximum payable	£941.22 per year

Exemption if pensionable age reached by 6 April 1992
Income tax relief allowed on 50% of Class 4 Contributions
Maximum relief (to be added to personal allowances): £470.61 per year

National Insurance Contributions
1991/92

Income limits

	Weekly	Monthly	Yearly
Lower earnings limit	£52.00	£225.00	£2,704
Upper earnings limit	£390.00	£1,690.00	£20,280

Class 1 Contributions
Standard rate (applying to all earnings)

Weekly earnings	Not contracted out		Contracted out		Employer	
	Employee	Employer	Employee On 1st £52	Remainder	On 1st £52	Remainder
£52.00 - £84.99	9%*	4.6%	2%	7%	4.6%	0.8%
£85.00 - £129.99	9%*	6.6%	2%	7%	6.6%	2.8%
£130.00 - £184.99	9%*	8.6%	2%	7%	8.6%	4.8%
£185.00 - £390.00	9%*	10.4%	2%	7%	10.4%	6.6% up to £390
Over £390.00	9%*	10.4%	2%	7%	10.4%	10.4% over £390
* but with a rate of only 2% on the first £52 of earnings	on £390	on all earnings	up to overall limit £390		on all earnings	

Reduced rates

	Employee	Employer
Married women and widows with valid certificate of election:	3.85%	As in above columns
Men over 65 and women over 60	nil	As in not contracted out column
Children under 16	nil	nil

Class 2 Contributions

Self-employed persons	£5.15 per week
Share fishermen's rate	£6.20 per week
Small earnings exemption	£2,900 per year

None payable by men over 65 or women over 60

Class 3 Contributions

Voluntary contributions   £5.05 per week
Not payable if pensionable age reached during year of assessment

Class 4 Contributions

Self-employed (added to Class 2)   6.3% on profits or gains between £5,900 and £20,280 per year
Maximum payable   £905.94 per year
Exemption if pensionable age reached by 6 April 1991
Income tax relief allowed on 50% of Class 4 Contributions
Maximum relief (to be added to personal allowances): £452.97 per year

National Insurance Contributions 1990/91

Income limits

	Weekly	Monthly	Yearly
Lower earnings limit	£46.00	£200.00	£2,392
Upper earnings limit	£350.00	£1,517.00	£18,200

Class 1 Contributions
Standard rate (applying to all earnings)

Weekly earnings	Not contracted out Employee	Not contracted out Employer	Contracted out Employee On 1st £46	Contracted out Employee Remainder	Employer On 1st £46	Employer Remainder
£46.00 - £79.99	9%*	5%	2%	7%	5%	1.2%
£80.00 - £124.99	9%*	7%	2%	7%	7%	3.2%
£125.00 - £174.99	9%*	9%	2%	7%	9%	5.2%
£175.00 - £349.99	9%*	10.45%	2%	7%	10.45%	6.65% up to £350
Over £350.00	9%*	10.45%	2%	7%	10.45%	10.45% over £350
* but with a rate of only 2% on the first £46 of earnings	on £350	on all earnings	up to overall limit £350		on all earnings	

Reduced rates

	Employee	Employer
Married women and widows with valid certificate of election:	3.85%	As in above columns
Men over 65 and women over 60	nil	As in not contracted out column
Children under 16	nil	nil

Class 2 Contributions

Self-employed persons	£4.55 per week
Share fishermen's rate	£6.15 per week
Small earnings exemption	£2,600 per year

None payable by men over 65 or women over 60

Class 3 Contributions

Voluntary contributions	£4.45 per week

Not payable if pensionable age reached during year of assessment

Class 4 Contributions

Self-employed (added to Class 2)	6.3% on profits or gains between £5,450 and £18,200 per year
Maximum payable	£803.25 per year

Exemption if pensionable age reached by 6 April 1990
Income tax relief allowed on 50% of Class 4 Contributions
Maximum relief (to be added to personal allowances): £401.62 per year

National Insurance Contributions
1989/90
(new rates from 5.10.89 in brackets)

Income limits

	Weekly	Monthly	Yearly
Lower earnings limit	£43.00	£187.00	£2,236
Upper earnings limit	£325.00	£1,409.00	£16,900

Class 1 Contributions
Standard rate (applying to all earnings)

Weekly earnings	Not contracted out Employee	Employer	Contracted out Employee On 1st £43	Remainder	Employer On 1st £43	Remainder
£43.00 - £74.99	5%(9%*)	5%	5%(2%)	3%(7%)	5%	1.2%
£75.00 - £114.99	7%(9%*)	7%	7%(2%)	5%(7%)	7%	3.2%
£115.00 - £164.99	9%(9%*)	9%	9%(2%)	7%(7%)	9%	5.2%
£165.00 - £325.00	9%(9%*)	10.45%	9%(2%)	7%(7%)	10.45%	6.65% up to £325
Over £325.00	9%(9%*)	10.45%	9%(2%)	7%(7%)	10.45%	10.45% over £325
* but with a rate of only 2% on the first £43 of earnings	on £325	on all earnings	up to overall limit £325		on all earnings	

Reduced rates

	Employee	Employer
Married women and widows with valid certificate of election:	3.85%	As in above columns
Men over 65 and women over 60	nil	As in not contracted out column
Children under 16	nil	nil

Class 2 Contributions

Self-employed persons	£4.25 per week
Share fishermen's rate	£5.80 per week
Small earnings exemption	£2,350 per year

None payable by men over 65 or women over 60

Class 3 Contributions

Voluntary contributions   £4.15 per week
Not payable if pensionable age reached during year of assessment

Class 4 Contributions

Self-employed (added to Class 2)   6.3% on profits or gains between £5,050 and £16,900 per year
Maximum payable   £746.55 per year
Exemption if pensionable age reached by 6 April 1989
Income tax relief allowed on 50% of Class 4 Contributions
Maximum relief (to be added to personal allowances): £373.28 per year

National Insurance Contributions 1988/89

Income limits

	Weekly	Monthly	Yearly
Lower earnings limit	£41.00	£178.00	£2,132
Upper earnings limit	£305.00	£1,322.00	£15,860

Class 1 Contributions
Standard rate (applying to all earnings)

Weekly earnings	Not contracted out		Contracted out		Employer	
	Employee	Employer	Employee On 1st £41	Remainder	On 1st £41	Remainder
£41.00 -£69.99	5%	5%	5%	3%	5%	1.2%
£70.00 -£104.99	7%	7%	7%	5%	7%	3.2%
£105.00 -£154.99	9%	9%	9%	7%	9%	5.2%
£155.00 -£305.00	9%	10.45%	9%	7%	10.45%	6.65% up to £305
Over £305	9%	10.45%	9%	7%	10.45%	10.45% over £305
	on £305	on all earnings	up to overall limit £305		on all earnings	

Reduced rates

	Employee	Employer
Married women and widows with valid certificate of election:	3.85%	As in above columns
Men over 65 and women over 60	nil	As in not contracted out column
Children under 16	nil	nil

Class 2 Contributions

Self-employed persons	£4.05 per week
Share fishermen's rate	£6.55 per week
Small earnings exemption	£2,250 per year

None payable by men over 65 or women over 60

Class 3 Contributions

Voluntary contributions   £3.95 per week

Not payable if pensionable age reached during year of assessment

Class 4 Contributions

Self-employed (added to Class 2)   6.3% on profits or gains between £4,750 and £15,860 per year

Maximum payable   £699.93 per year

Exemption if pensionable age reached by 6 April 1988

Income tax relief allowed on 50% of Class 4 Contributions

Maximum relief (to be added to personal allowances):   £349.97 per year

National Insurance Contributions
1987/88

Income limits

	Weekly	Monthly	Yearly
Lower earnings limit	£39.00	£169.00	£2,028
Upper earnings limit	£295.00	£1,279.00	£15,340

Class 1 Contributions

Standard rate (applying to all earnings)

Weekly earnings	Not contracted out Employee	Employer	Contracted out Employee On 1st £39	Remainder	Employer On 1st £39	Remainder
£39.00 -£64.99	5%	5%	5%	2.85%	5%	0.9%
£65.00 -£99.99	7%	7%	7%	4.85%	7%	2.9%
£100.00 -£149.99	9%	9%	9%	6.85%	9%	4.9%
£150.00 -£295.00	9%	10.45%	9%	6.85%	10.45%	6.35%
Over £295	9% on £295	10.45% on all earnings	9% up to overall limit £295	6.85%	10.45% on all earnings	6.35% up to £295 10.45% over £295

Reduced rates

	Employee	Employer
Married women and widows with valid certificate of election:	3.85%	As in above columns
Men over 65 and women over 60	nil	As in not contracted out column
Children under 16	nil	nil

Class 2 Contributions

Self-employed persons	£3.85 per week
Share fishermen's rate	£6.55 per week
Small earnings exemption	£2,125 per year
None payable by men over 65 or women over 60	

Class 3 Contributions

Voluntary contributions	£3.75 per week
Not payable if pensionable age reached during year of assessment	

Class 4 Contributions

Self-employed (added to Class 2)	6.3% on profits or gains between £4,590 and £15,340 per year
Maximum payable	£677.25 per year
Exemption if pensionable age reached by 6 April 1987	
Income tax relief allowed on 50% of Class 4 Contributions	
Maximum relief (to be added to personal allowances):	£338.62 per year

Stamp Duties

To be abolished on property other than land and buildings from a date to be announced (intended to be at the same time as the abolition of duty on shares, which is not likely to be before April 1993)

Fixed duties

Surviving fixed duties (SA 1891, Sch 1 and ss 83 & 84 FA 1985) include:

Head/description	Duty
Conveyance or transfer of any other kind *	50p **
Death: varying dispositions and appropriations	50p **
Declaration of any use or trust (not being a Will)	50p
Duplicates or counterparts	50p ***
Instruments effecting exchange or excambion (in any other case) *	50p
Instruments effecting partition or division (in any other case)*	50p
Instruments effecting release or renunciation (in any other case) *	50p
Surrender (not on sale) *	50p
Transfers in connection with divorce etc	50p **

* Documents that effect sales are chargeable with *ad valorem* duty
** Unless a duly certified exempt instrument (see table below)
*** Or, if it is less, the same duty as the original

Repealed fixed duty heads (s 85 FA 1985) include:

- agreement and contract made or entered into pursuant to the Highways Act;
- appointment of a new trustee and appointment in execution of a power of any property;
- covenant (any separate deed of covenant not being chargeable with *ad valorem* duty etc);
- deed of any kind whatsoever (not liable to other duties);
- letter or power of attorney;
- revocation of any use or trust of any property by any writing (not being a Will).

Ad valorem stamp duties

Consideration[†] for a conveyance or transfer on sale of property (other than stock and marketable securities), or premium for a lease (SA 1891, Sch 1 and especially s 55(1) FA 1963)

(1) Consideration or premium - Exceeds	Does not exceed	(2) Instrument certified at £30,000 or £250,000 *	(3) Instrument not certified **
£	£		£
	50	nil	0.50
50	100	nil	1.00
100	150	nil	1.50
150	200	nil	2.00
200	250	nil	2.50
250	300	nil	3.00
300	350	nil	3.50
350	400	nil	4.00
400	450	nil	4.50
450	500	nil	5.00
500	30,000	nil	1.00 per £100 or part of £100
30,000	250,000	nil	1.00 per £100 or part of £100
250,000			1.00 per £100 or part of £100

* An instrument which is "certified" at a particular amount (£30,000 from 13/20.3.84) (or £250,000 from 20.12.91 to 19.8.92) is one which contains a statement (known as a certificate of value) certifying that the transaction effected by the instrument does not form part of a larger transaction or series of transactions in respect of which the amount or value, or aggregate amount or value, of the consideration exceeds that amount. For the purpose of determining the amount at which an instrument is to be certified the consideration for any sale or contract or agreement for the sale of goods, wares or merchandise should be disregarded (except where the instrument is itself an actual conveyance or transfer of the goods, wares or merchandise, with or without other property).
** There is no provision for the certification of leases at a yearly rate of rent exceeding £300 (or £2,500 from 20.12.91 to 19.8.92), and all such instruments are chargeable with the duty shown in Column (3), or of transfers of stock and marketable securities.
† For instruments executed on or after 1.8.91 consideration is the VAT inclusive amount (i) on the sale of a new non-domestic building; (ii) where the VAT exemption has been waived, or (iii) where the VAT exemption has not been waived but there are payments to which an election could still apply.

Consideration for a transfer on sale of stock and marketable securities
(SA 1891 Sch 1 and especially s 55(1A) FA 1963)
To be abolished for transactions on or after a date (not likely to be before April 1993) to be announced

Rate of duty - 0.5% (expressed as 50p per £100 or part of £100) from 27.10.86.

Leases (including, from 20.3.84, agreements for leases)
Premiums (see the table above)
Rents†:

Leases up to 7 years (or where an indefinite term)	
Rent† p.a.	Duty
£ 0 - 500	nil
Over £500	50p per £50 or part of £50 *

* A lease of any furnished dwelling house or apartment for a term less than a year where the rent† exceeds £500 bears duty at £1.

Leases over 7 years				
Rent† p.a. Over	Up to	Term (years) - 7 + to 35	35 + to 100	100 +
0 -	5	10p	60p	120p
5 -	10	20p	120p	240p
10 -	15	30p	180p	360p
15 -	20	40p	240p	480p
20 -	25	50p	(£) 3	(£) 6
25 -	50	100p	6	12
50 -	75	150p	9	18
75 -	100	(£) 2	12	24
100 -	150	3	18	36
150 -	200	4	24	48
200 -	250	5	30	60
250 -	300	6	36	72
300 -	350	7	42	84
350 -	400	8	48	96
400 -	450	9	54	108
450 -	500	10	60	120
500 + (for every £50 or part of £50)		1	6	12

† For instruments executed on or after 1.8.91 rent is the VAT inclusive amount where (a) the VAT exemption has been waived or has not been waived but there are payments to which an election could still apply; and (b) the VAT is itself treated as rent under the lease. (In other cases see SP11/91.)

Exempt instruments

Certain documents dated on or after 1.5.87 are exempt from duty, subject to being duly certified by the transferor or grantor, or a solicitor or authorised agent. A suggested form of words is:

"I/We hereby certify that this instrument falls within category [see Table below] in the Schedule to the Stamp Duty (Exempt Instruments) Regulations 1987."

An authorised agent must also state his capacity, confirm he is authorised and that he has knowledge of the facts of the transaction.

Category Description
A   The vesting of property subject to a trust in the trustees of the trust on the appointment of a new trustee, or in the continuing trustees on the retirement of a trustee.
B   The conveyance or transfer of property the subject of a specific devise or legacy to the beneficiary named in the Will (or his nominee).
C   The conveyance or transfer of property which forms part of an intestate's estate to the person entitled on intestacy (or his nominee).
D   The appropriation of property within s 84(4) FA 1985 (death: appropriation in satisfaction of a general legacy of money) or s 84(5) or (7) of that Act (death: appropriation in satisfaction of any interest of surviving spouse and in Scotland also of any interest of issue).
E   The conveyance or transfer of property which forms part of the residuary estate of a testator to a beneficiary (or his nominee) entitled solely by virtue of his entitlement under the Will.

F The conveyance or transfer of property out of a settlement in or towards satisfaction of a beneficiary's interest, not being an interest acquired for money or money's worth, being a conveyance or transfer constituting a distribution of property in accordance with the provisions of the settlement.

G The conveyance or transfer of property on and in consideration only of marriage to a party to the marriage (or his nominee) or to trustees to be held on the terms of a settlement made in consideration only of the marriage.

H The conveyance or transfer of property within s 83(1) FA 1985 (transfers in connection with divorce etc).

I The conveyance or transfer by the liquidator of property which formed part of the assets of the company in liquidation to a shareholder of that company (or his nominee) in or towards satisfaction of the shareholder's rights on a winding-up.

J The grant in fee simple of an easement in or over land for no consideration in money or money's worth.

K The grant of a servitude for no consideration in money or money's worth.

L The conveyance or transfer of property operating as a voluntary disposition *inter vivos* for no consideration in money or money's worth nor any consideration referred to in s 57 SA 1891 (conveyance in consideration of a debt etc).

M The conveyance or transfer of property by an instrument within s 84(1) FA 1985 (death: varying disposition).

Stamp Duty Reliefs

- s 42 FA 1930 (relief on certain transfers between associated companies)
- s 75 FA 1986 (relief on acquisition of undertaking in scheme of reconstruction)
- s 76 FA 1986 (relief on acquisition of undertaking: further provisions)
- s 77 FA 1986 (relief on certain share for share acquisitions)
- s 129 FA 1982 (exemption on grants, transfers to charities etc)

(The Stamp Office, Adjudication Section address is given on page 4.)

Stamp Duty Reserve Tax

Applies from 26.10.86.

To be abolished for transactions on or after a date (not likely to be before April 1993) to be announced.

Principal rate of duty - 0.5% (expressed as 50p for every £100 or part of £100).

SDRT liability will most frequently arise where a person:
(a) buys a security and resells it within the same Stock Exchange account;
(b) buys renounceable letters of allotment or acceptance;
(c) buys shares which are registered in the name of a nominee, who acts both for the seller and the purchaser;
(d) buys shares which are resold before being transferred into his name.
(e) bed and breakfast transactions.
(Extracted from Notes for Guidance)

Capital Duty

Abolished for transactions on or after 16.3.88
Rate of duty - 1% (expressed as £1 per £100 or part of £100) up to 15.3.88.

Value Added Tax

The completion of the EC Single Market on 1.1.93 and the removal of fiscal frontier controls will result in some fundamental changes to the arrangements for the collection and control of VAT due on intra-Community transactions.

Rates (ss 9 & 16 VATA 1983)

	Type of supply	Rate from 18.6.79 - 31.3.91 15%	Rate from 1.4.91
		Standard rated	17.5%*
	Zero rated	0%	0%

*From 1.4.91 the VAT fraction of the VAT inclusive price is 7/47

Zero-rated supplies (s 16 & Sch 5 VATA 1983)

Group	Description of supplies
1	Food
2	Sewerage services and water (revised from 1.7.90)
3	Books etc
4	Talking books for the blind and handicapped and wireless sets for the blind
[5	Newspaper advertisements (before 1.5.85)]
[6	News services (before 1.4.89)]
7	Fuel and power for domestic or charity use (before 1.7.90, fuel and power)
8	Construction of dwellings etc (before 1.4.89, construction of buildings etc)
8A	Protected buildings (from 1.6.84)
9	International services
10	Transport
11	Caravans and houseboats
12	Gold
13	Bank notes
14	Drugs, medicines, aids for the handicapped etc
15	Imports, exports etc
16	Charities etc
17	Clothing and footwear

Exempt supplies (s 17, s 35A, Schs 6 & 6A VATA 1983)

Group	Description of supplies
1	Land (revised from 1.4.89 and also from 1.1.92)
2	Insurance
3	Postal services
4	Betting, gaming and lotteries
5	Finance
6	Education
7	Health and welfare (before 1.1.86, health)
8	Burial and cremation
9	Trade unions and professional bodies
10	Sports competitions
11	Works of art, etc
12	Fund-raising events by charities and other qualifying bodies (before 1.4.89, fund-raising events)

"Relevant services" (s 7 & Sch 3 VATA 1983)

These are for reverse charge purposes (s 7 VATA 1983) and zero-rating purposes (Sch 5 Group 9)

Para	Description of services
1	Transfers and assignments of copyright, patents, licences, trade marks and similar rights
2	Advertising services
3	Services of consultants, engineers, consultancy bureaux, lawyers, accountants and other similar services; data processing and provision of information (but excluding from this head any services relating to land)
4	Acceptance of any obligation to refrain from pursuing or exercising, in whole or part, any business activity or any such rights referred to in para 1 above
5	Banking, financial and insurance services (including reinsurance, but not including the provision of safe deposit facilities)
6	The supply of staff
6A	The letting on hire of goods other than means of transport (from 1.7.85)
7	The services rendered by one person to another in procuring for the other any of the services mentioned in 1 - 6A above.

Registration limits (s 2(5) and Sch 1 para 1 VATA 1983): Summary

A person must register for VAT if the value of his taxable supplies will exceed or has exceeded one of the limits in the following table:

| Dates | Value of taxable supplies | | | |
| | Future: In next 12 months will exceed | Past: After end of any quarter exceeds * (i) | After end of any four quarters exceeds ** (ii) | After end of any month if past 12 months exceed *** |
	£	£	£	£
18.3.87 - 15.3.88	21,300	7,250	21,300	N/A
16.3.88 - 14.3.89	22,100	7,500	22,100	N/A
15.3.89 - 20.3.90	23,600	8,000	23,600	N/A
21.3.90 - 19.3.91	N/A	N/A	N/A	25,400
20.3.91 - 10.3.92	N/A	N/A	N/A	35,000
11.3.92 –	N/A	N/A	N/A	36,600

* Unless taxable supplies in that quarter and the next three will not exceed the limit in column (ii).
** Unless (from 18.3.87 onwards) taxable supplies in the next four quarters will not exceed £20,300 (18.3.87 - 15.3.88); £21,100 (16.3.88 - 14.3.89); or £22,600 (15.3.89 - 20.3.90.)
*** Or at any time if value in next 30 days will exceed the limit.

De-registration limits (s 2(5) and Sch 1 para 2 VATA 1983): Summary

A person can apply for voluntary de-registration if the value of taxable supplies will not exceed the future limit in the following table. Previously, there was an alternative historical limit:

| Dates limit(s) applicable | Value of taxable supplies | |
| | Future: In next 12 months will not exceed | Past: After end of any quarter or accounting period, in each of the two previous years, did not exceed ** |
	£	£
1.6.86 - 14.5.87	19,500	20,500
15.5.87 - 31.5.88	20,300 *	N/A
1.6.88 - 31.5.89	21,100 *	N/A
1.6.89 - 30.4..90	22,600*	N/A
1.6.90 - 30.4.91	24,400*	N/A
1.5.91 - 30.4.92	33,600*	N/A
1.5.92 –	35,100*	N/A

* Unless (from 15.5.87) attributable to ceasing taxable supplies or suspending making taxable supplies for at least 30 days.
** Unless (before 15.5.87) taxable supplies would exceed that amount in the next 12 months.

Fuel for private use (s 9 and Sch 6 FA 1986): Scale consideration

| Accounting period: Starting after | Cylinder capacity - cc | Three months Business use (miles) | | | | One month Business use (miles) | | | |
| | | Under 4,500 | | 4,500 or more | | Under 1,500 | | 1,500 or more | |
		Petrol	Diesel	Petrol	Diesel	Petrol	Diesel	Petrol	Diesel
6.4.87	0 - 1,400	£120	£120	£60	£60	£40	£40	£20	£20
	1,401* - 2,000	£150	£150	£75	£75	£50	£50	£25	£25
	2,001 or over	£225	£225	£113	£113	£75	£75	£38	£38
6.4.92	0 - 1,400	£125	£115	£63	£58	£42	£38	£21	£19
	1,401* - 2,000	£158	£115	£79	£58	£53	£38	£26	£19
* ie over 1,400	2,001 or over	£235	£148	£118	£74	£78	£49	£39	£25

The European Community

Member States (VAT territory)	Date of entry (if not 1.1.58)

Belgium ....
Denmark (excluding Greenland and the Faroe Islands) 1.1.73
Federal Republic of Germany (excluding the Island of Heligoland and the territory of Büsingen)
France (excluding the overseas departments)
Greece (excluding Agio Oros) 1.1.81
The Republic of Ireland 1.1.73
Italy (excluding Livigno, Campione d'Italia and the Italian water of Lake Lugano)

Luxembourg
Netherlands
Portugal 1.1.86
(1.1.89 for certain VAT purposes)
Spain (including the Balearic Islands but excluding the Canary Islands, Ceuta and Melilla) 1.1.86
United Kingdom (the Isle of Man deemed part of the UK 1.1.73

The following territories, in particular, are not in the EC: Andorra, Channel Islands, Liechtenstein, Monaco, San Marino and The Vatican.

HM Customs & Excise Notices

This is a list of VAT Notices and leaflets (excluding VAT Notes and VAT Information Sheets), and some other HM Customs & Excise Notices. Notices appear in *italic type*; Leaflets in plain type:

Notice / leaflet no.	Title	Notice / leaflet no.	Title
101	*Duty Deferment*	700/30/89	Default surcharge appeals
119	*Importation or Retention of a Private Motor Vehicle without payment of Customs Duty or Tax*	700/31/86	Pawnbrokers: Disposals of pledged goods
		700/33/90	Government-funded training programmes and schemes to assist the unemployed*
120	*Importation of Private Motor vehicles*	700/34/88	Supplies of staff, including directors and other office-holders
221	*Inward Processing Relief*		
232	*Customs Warehousing*	700/35/88	Business gifts
251 & 252	*Valuation of imported goods for customs purposes - directions for completing valuation declarations and statements: VAT and Trade statistics*	700/36/88	Dealer loader promotional schemes
		700/40/88	Persistent misdeclaration penalty
		700/41/88	Late registration: penalties and reasonable excuse
483	*Import and Export Clearance Procedures*	700/42/90	Serious misdeclaration penalty
		700/43/90	Default interest
700	*The VAT Guide (Revised 1 August 1991)*	700/44/90	Barristers and advocates: tax point on ceasing to practise
700/1/91	Should I be registered for VAT?		
700/2A/91	The VAT group treatment requirements	700/45/91	How to correct errors you find on your VAT returns
700/3/91	Registration for VAT: Corporate bodies organised in Divisions	701/1/92	Charities
700/4/87	Overseas traders and United Kingdom VAT	701/5/90	Clubs and Associations
		701/6/86	Donated medical and scientific equipment*
700/5/85	Hire-purchase and conditional sale; re-possession and transfers of agreements	701/7/86	Aids for handicapped persons (amendment 1988)
700/7/81	Business promotion schemes		
700/8/84	Containers (including returnable containers) for which a separate charge is made	701/8/85	Postage stamps and philatelic supplies
		701/9/85	Terminal markets: dealing with commodities (amendment 1987)
700/9/87	Transfer of a business as a going concern	701/10/85	Printed and similar matter*
700/10/84	Processing and repair of goods and supplies of exchange units	701/12/89	Sales of antiques, works of art etc from stately homes
700/11/91	Should I cancel my registration?	701/13/89	Gaming and amusement machines (amendment 1990)
700/12/92	Filling in your VAT return*		
700/13/92	VAT publications	701/14/89	Food*
700/14/86	Video cassette films: rental and part exchange	701/15/87	Animal feeding stuffs
		701/16/90	Sewerage services and water
700/15/91	The Ins and Outs of VAT (August 1991) (erratum slip)	701/19/90	Fuel and power
		701/20/89	Caravans and houseboats
700/17/83	Funded pension schemes	701/21/87	Gold and gold coins (amendment 1990)
700/18/91	Relief from VAT on bad debts	701/22/84	Tools for the manufacture of goods for export
700/21/91	Keeping records and accounts		
700/22/89	Admissions	701/23/90	Protective boots and helmets
700/24/88	Delivery charges	701/24/84	Parking facilities (amendment 1989)
700/25/84	Taxis and hire cars	701/25/86	Pet food
700/26/91	Visits by VAT officers	701/26/84	Betting and gaming
700/28/85	Services supplied by estate agents	701/27/90	Bingo
		701/28/84	Lotteries

* *revision or amendment expected*

Notice / leaflet no.	Title
701/29/85	Finance (amendment 1990)
701/30/87	Education
701/31/88	Health (amendment 1990)
701/32/85	Burial and cremation
701/33/89	Trade unions, professional bodies and learned societies
701/34/89	Competitions in sport and physical recreation
701/35/84	Youth Clubs
701/36/86	Insurance (amendment September 1986, 1988 and January and May 1991)
701/37/84	Live animals
701/38/89	Seeds and plants (amendment September 1991)
701/39/90	VAT liability law (amendment April 1991)
701/40/91	Abattoirs
701/41/90	Sponsorship
702	*Imports and warehoused goods (1988)*
702/1/88	Importing goods on which VAT has already been paid in the EC
702/3/91	Repayment of import VAT to shipping agents and freight forwarders
702/4/89	Importing computer software
702/5/89	Mares temporarily exported for covering abroad: reimportation with or without foals at foot
702/6/91	Import VAT certificates
703	*Exports (1987) (amendment 1990)**
703/1/89	Freight containers supplied for export
703/2/87	Sailaway boats supplied for export
703/3/87	VAT-free purchases of sailaway boats
704	*Retail exports (1990 and amendment July 1991)*
704/1/85	VAT refunds for visitors to the United Kingdom (amendments October 1985, 1987, 1988, 1990 and 1991)
704/2/92	Traveller's guide to the retail export scheme
705	*Personal exports of new motor vehicles (1991)*
706	*Partial exemption (1990)*
706/1/91	Self supply of stationery
706/2/90	Capital goods scheme: input tax on computers, land and buildings acquired for use in your business
708/1/90	Protected buildings (listed buildings and scheduled monuments)
708/2/90	Construction industry (and erratum slip October 1990)
708/4/90	Construction: VAT certificates for residential or charity buildings
709/1/87	Industrial, staff and public sector catering
709/2/91	Catering and take-away food
709/3/90	Hotels and holiday accommodation (amendment February 1991)
709/4/88	Package holidays and other holiday services
709/5/88	Tour operators' margin scheme (amendment April 1991)
710/1/91	Theatrical agents and Nett Acts
710/2/83	Agencies providing nurses and nursing auxiliaries
710/3/83	Private investigators: Expenses charged to clients
711	*Second-hand cars (1990)*
711/1/90	VAT and the second-hand car scheme - a guide to the records for the registered dealer
712	*Second-hand works of art, antiques and collectors' pieces (1990)*
712/2/90	Second-hand works of art, antiques and collectors' pieces

Notice / leaflet no.	Title
713	*Second-hand motor-cycles (1990)*
714	*Young children's clothing and footwear (1986 and amendments September 1986, 1988 (cancelled) and 1990)*
717	*Second-hand caravans and motor caravans (1990)*
719	*VAT Refunds for "do it yourself" housebuilders (1991)*
720	*Second-hand boats and outboard motors (1985 and amendment 1990)*
721	*Second-hand aircraft (1985 and amendment 1990)*
722	*Second-hand electronic organs (1985 and amendments 1987 and 1990)*
723	*Refunds of VAT in the EC and other countries (1988 and amendment 1989)*
724	*Second-hand firearms (1985 and amendments September 1985 and 1990)*
726	*Second-hand horses and ponies (1985 and amendments September 1985 and 1990)*
727	*Retail schemes (1987 and amendments October 1988 and December 1991)*
727/1/87	Retail Florists - Accounting for VAT on Interflora and Teleflorist transactions
727/6/87	Choosing your Retail Scheme*
727/7/87	How to Work Scheme A
727/8/87	How to Work Scheme B
727/8A/87	How to Work Scheme B Adaptation 1
727/8B/87	How to Work Scheme B Adaptation 2
727/9/87	How to Work Scheme C
727/10/87	How to Work Scheme D
727/11/87	How to Work Scheme E
727/11A/87	How to Work Scheme E Adaptation 1
727/12/87	How to Work Scheme F
727/13/87	How to Work Scheme G
727/14/90	How to Work Scheme H
727/15/90	How to Work Scheme J
731	*Cash Accounting (1991)*
732	*Annual Accounting (1988 and amendment May 1991)*
741	*International services (1986 and amendments April 1987 and June 1987)*
742A	*Property development (1990 and amendments 1990 and January 1992)*
742B	*Property ownership (1990 and amendments May 1991 and 2 in January 1992)*
742/1/90	Letting of facilities for sport and physical recreation
742/2/90	Sporting rights
744	*Passenger transport, international freight, ships and aircraft (1984 and amendment November 1984) **
748	*Extra-statutory concessions (1991)*
749	*Local authorities and similar bodies (1990)*
Leaflet	Appeals and applications to the Tribunals (1991)

* Revision or amendment expected

Court Special Account Interest Rates

The special account was formerly known as the Short Term Investment Account. Its rates are used for calculating interest on special damages, primarily in personal injury cases. Since:

Date	%
1 January 1980	15.00
1 January 1981	12.50
1 December 1981	15.00
1 March 1982	14.00
1 July 1982	13.00
1 April 1983	12.50
1 April 1984	12.00
1 August 1986	11.50
1 January 1987	12.25
1 April 1987	11.75
1 November 1987	11.25
1 December 1987	11.00
1 May 1988	9.50
1 August 1988	11.00
1 November 1988	12.25
1 January 1989	13.00
1 November 1989	14.25
1 April 1991	12.00
1 October 1991	10.25

Special Damage Interest Table

The left-hand column shows the month from the first day of which interest is assumed to run. The right-hand columns show the percentage interest accumulated from the first day of each month to 1 April 1992.

Continued use may be made of this table by adding to the figures therein $1/365$th of the special account rate from 1 April 1992 onwards. Since June 1987 this interest is paid daily on a $1/365$th basis, even in a leap year.

	1981	1982	1983	1984	1985	1986	1987	1988	1989	1990	1991	1992
January	139.67	126.95	113.30	100.67	88.55	76.55	64.75	52.99	42.13	28.92	14.67	2.56
February	138.60	125.68	112.19	99.61	87.53	75.53	63.72	52.06	41.02	27.71	13.46	1.68
March	137.64	124.53	111.19	98.62	86.61	74.61	62.78	51.18	40.03	26.62	12.37	0.87
April	136.58	123.34	110.09	97.56	85.59	73.59	61.74	50.25	38.92	25.41	11.16	
May	135.56	122.19	109.06	96.58	84.60	72.60	60.77	49.34	37.85	24.23	10.17	
June	134.49	121.00	108.00	95.56	83.58	71.58	59.77	48.54	36.75	23.02	9.15	
July	133.47	119.85	106.97	94.58	82.60	70.60	58.81	47.76	35.68	21.85	8.16	
August	132.41	118.74	105.91	93.56	81.58	69.58	57.81	46.95	34.58	20.64	7.14	
September	131.34	117.64	104.85	92.55	80.56	68.60	56.81	46.01	33.47	19.43	6.13	
October	130.32	116.57	103.82	91.57	79.57	67.66	55.86	45.11	32.40	18.26	5.14	
November	129.25	115.47	102.76	90.55	78.55	66.68	54.85	44.18	31.30	17.05	4.27	
December	128.23	114.40	101.73	89.57	77.57	65.73	53.92	43.16	30.13	15.88	3.43	

Judgment Debt Interest Rates

(pursuant to s 17 Judgments Act 1838)

	Date	%
Before	20 April 1971	4.00
Since	20 April 1971	7.50
	1 March 1977	10.00
	3 December 1979	12.50
	9 June 1980	15.00
	8 June 1982	14.00
	10 November 1982	12.00
	16 April 1985	15.00

Clearing Bank Base Rates

Friday	Ave %	Friday	Ave %	Friday	Ave %
1982		**1985**		**1988**	
29 January	14.00*	11 January	10.50	5 February	9.00
26 February	13.50	18 January	12.00	18 March	8.50
19 March	13.00	1 February	14.00	15 April	8.0
11 June	12.50	22 March	13.50	20 May	7.50
16 July	12.00	29 March	13.25 (13.00-13.50)	3 June	8.00
6 August	11.50	4 April	13 1/8 (13.00-13.25)	10 June	8.50
20 August	11.00	12 April	12 7/8 (12.75-13.00)	24 June	9.00
3 September	10.50	19 April	12 5/8 (12.50-12.75)	1 July	9.50
8 October	10.00	14 June	12.50	8 July	10.00
15 October	9.50	19 July	12.00	22 July	10.50
5 November	9.00	2 August	11.50	12 August	11.00
26 November	9.50 (9-10)			26 August	12.00
3 December	10.25 (10-10.25)	**1986**		25 November	13.00
		10 January	12.50		
1983		21 March	11.50	**1989**	
14 January	11.00	11 April	11.00	26 May	14.00
18 March	10.50	18 April	10.50	6 October	15.00
15 April	10.00	30 May	10.00		
17 June	9.50	17 October	11.00	**1990**	
7 October	9.00			12 October	14.00
		1987			
1984		13 March	10.50	**1991**	
9 March	8.94	20 March	10.00	15 February	13.50
16 March	8.56	1 May	9.50	1 March	13.00
11 May	9.13	15 May	9.00	22 March	12.50
29 June	9.25	7 August	10.00	12 April	12.00
13 July	12.00	30 October	9.50	24 May	11.50
10 August	11.00	6 November	9.00	12 July	11.00
24 August	10.50	4 December	8.50	6 September	10.50
9 November	10.00				
23 November	9 5/8 (9.50-9.75)				

*The rate had been at 14.5% since late 1981. Note: These lists are based on tables published in the Bank of England Quarterly Bulletin. The changes are shown as on the last working day each week, although they may have taken place earlier in certain weeks.

Multiplier Tables

The figures contained in the tables have been produced by the Government Actuary's Department. The basis of the multipliers set out therein is that the lump sum award for future loss of earnings or pension will be invested and yield income, but that over the period in question the plaintiff will gradually reduce the capital sum so that at the end of the period it is exhausted. Currently the courts use multipliers which implicitly assume a discount rate of between 4% and 5%. The tables take into account population mortality but not other risks to life such as ill health or unemployment.

Loss of earnings to age 65 (males)				Loss of pension from age 65 (males)				Loss of earnings to age 60 (females)				Loss of pension from age 60 (females)			
Age	4%	4.5%	5%	Age	4%	4.5%	5%	Age	4%	4.5%	5%	Age	4%	4.5%	5%
20	20.4	19.0	17.7	20	1.1	.9	.7	-	-	-	-	-	-	-	-
21	20.2	18.8	17.6	21	1.2	.9	.7	16	20.7	19.2	17.9	16	2.1	1.6	1.3
22	20.0	18.6	17.4	22	1.2	1.0	.8	17	20.5	19.0	17.7	17	2.2	1.7	1.3
23	19.8	18.5	17.3	23	1.3	1.0	.8	18	20.3	18.9	17.6	18	2.3	1.8	1.4
24	19.6	18.3	17.1	24	1.3	1.1	.8	19	20.1	18.7	17.5	19	2.4	1.8	1.5
25	19.4	18.1	17.0	25	1.4	1.1	.9	20	19.9	18.5	17.3	20	2.5	1.9	1.5
26	19.2	17.9	16.8	26	1.4	1.1	.9	21	19.6	18.4	17.2	21	2.6	2.0	1.6
27	18.9	17.7	16.7	27	1.5	1.2	1.0	22	19.4	18.2	17.0	22	2.7	2.1	1.7
28	18.7	17.5	16.5	28	1.6	1.3	1.0	23	19.2	18.0	16.9	23	2.8	2.2	1.8
29	18.4	17.3	16.3	29	1.6	1.3	1.1	24	18.9	17.8	16.7	24	2.9	2.3	1.9
30	18.2	17.1	16.1	30	1.7	1.4	1.1	25	18.7	17.5	16.5	25	3.0	2.4	2.0
31	17.9	16.8	15.9	31	1.8	1.4	1.2	26	18.4	17.3	16.3	26	3.1	2.5	2.1
32	17.6	16.6	15.7	32	1.8	1.5	1.2	27	18.2	17.1	16.1	27	3.2	2.6	2.2
33	17.3	16.3	15.5	33	1.9	1.6	1.3	28	17.9	16.8	15.9	28	3.4	2.8	2.3
34	17.0	16.1	15.2	34	2.0	1.6	1.4	29	17.6	16.6	15.7	29	3.5	2.9	2.4
35	16.7	15.8	15.0	35	2.1	1.7	1.4	30	17.3	16.3	15.5	30	3.6	3.0	2.5
36	16.4	15.5	14.7	36	2.1	1.8	1.5	31	16.9	16.0	15.2	31	3.8	3.2	2.6
37	16.0	15.2	14.5	37	2.2	1.9	1.6	32	16.6	15.8	15.0	32	3.9	3.3	2.8
38	15.7	14.9	14.2	38	2.3	2.0	1.7	33	16.3	15.4	14.7	33	4.1	3.5	2.9
39	15.3	14.6	13.9	39	2.4	2.1	1.8	34	15.9	15.1	14.4	34	4.3	3.6	3.1
40	14.9	14.2	13.6	40	2.5	2.2	1.9	35	15.5	14.8	14.1	35	4.5	3.8	3.2
41	14.5	13.9	13.3	41	2.6	2.3	2.0	36	15.2	14.5	13.8	36	4.6	3.9	3.4
42	14.1	13.5	12.9	42	2.7	2.4	2.1	37	14.8	14.1	13.5	37	4.8	4.1	3.5
43	13.7	13.1	12.6	43	2.9	2.5	2.2	38	14.4	13.7	13.2	38	5.0	4.3	3.7
44	13.3	12.8	12.3	44	3.0	2.6	2.3	39	13.9	13.3	12.8	39	5.2	4.5	3.9
45	12.9	12.4	11.9	45	3.1	2.7	2.4	40	13.5	12.9	12.4	40	5.4	4.7	4.1
46	12.4	11.9	11.5	46	3.3	2.9	2.5	41	13.0	12.5	12.1	41	5.7	5.0	4.3
47	11.9	11.5	11.1	47	3.4	3.0	2.7	42	12.5	12.1	11.7	42	5.9	5.2	4.6
48	11.5	11.1	10.7	48	3.6	3.2	2.8	43	12.1	11.6	11.2	43	6.2	5.4	4.8
49	11.0	10.6	10.3	49	3.7	3.3	3.0	44	11.5	11.2	10.8	44	6.4	5.7	5.0
50	10.5	10.1	9.8	50	3.9	3.5	3.2	45	11.0	10.7	10.3	45	6.7	6.0	5.3
51	9.9	9.6	9.4	51	4.1	3.7	3.3	46	10.5	10.2	9.9	46	7.0	6.2	5.6
52	9.4	9.1	8.9	52	4.3	3.9	3.5	47	9.9	9.6	9.4	47	7.3	6.5	5.9
53	8.8	8.6	8.4	53	4.5	4.1	3.8	48	9.3	9.1	8.8	48	7.6	6.9	6.2
54	8.2	8.1	7.9	54	4.7	4.3	4.0	49	8.7	8.5	8.3	49	7.9	7.2	6.5
55	7.7	7.5	7.3	55	5.0	4.6	4.2	50	8.1	7.9	7.7	50	8.3	7.6	6.9
56	7.0	6.9	6.8	56	5.2	4.8	4.5	51	7.4	7.2	7.1	51	8.7	7.9	7.3
57	6.4	6.3	6.2	57	5.5	5.1	4.8	52	6.7	6.6	6.5	52	9.1	8.3	7.7
58	5.7	5.6	5.5	58	5.8	5.4	5.1	53	6.0	5.9	5.8	53	9.5	8.7	8.1
59	5.0	5.0	4.9	59	6.2	5.8	5.4	54	5.2	5.2	5.1	54	9.9	9.2	8.5
60	4.3	4.2	4.2	60	6.5	6.2	5.8	55	4.5	4.4	4.4	55	10.4	9.7	9.0
61	3.5	3.5	3.5	61	6.9	6.6	6.3	56	3.6	3.6	3.6	56	10.8	10.2	9.5
62	2.7	2.7	2.7	62	7.4	7.0	6.7	57	2.8	2.8	2.8	57	11.4	10.7	10.1
63	1.9	1.9	1.9	63	7.9	7.5	7.2	58	1.9	1.9	1.9	58	11.9	11.3	10.7
64	1.0	1.0	1.0	64	8.4	8.1	7.8	59	1.0	1.0	1.0	59	12.5	11.9	11.3

Due dates of tax and table dates: summary

Tax	Due dates	Dates tax ought to have been paid (s 88 TMA 1970)	Table Dates (s 86(4) TMA 1970)
Schedule A	Later of 1 January in YA and 30 days after notice of assessment issued	1 January in YA	1 July following end of YA
Schedule C	30 days after notice of assessment issued		Last day of 6 months following due date (includes Sch D III public revenue)
Schedule D	Cases I, II & V (trades, professions): two equal payments on 1 Jan in YA and 1 July after YA (or, in either case, 30 days after notice of assessment issued if later) Cases III, IV & V (other than trades, professions) & VI: later of 1 Jan in YA and 30 days after notice issued	1 January in YA (or where instalments 1 January in YA and 1 July following)	1 July following end of YA(excludes Sch D III public revenue)
Schedule E	PAYE in YA or 14 days after issue of demand	1 January in YA	N/A
Higher rate income tax	Later of 1 Dec after YA and 30 days after notice issued	1 December in YA following the year tax is charged	1 June following 1 December used in calculating due date
Capital gains tax	Later of 1 Dec following end of YA and 30 days after notice issued	1 December in YA following the year tax is charged	1 June following 1 December used in calculating due date
Corporation tax ('Pay and File' planned to start in Oct 1993)	Generally later of 9 months after end of accounting period and 30 days after notice of assessment issued (longer for some companies trading before financial year 1965, until the 3rd accounting period starting after 16.3.87 - see TA 1988 Sch 30)	Generally 9 months from end of chargeable accounting period	Generally, last day of 6 months following due date
ACT	14 days after end of return period (31 March, 30 June, 30 September, 31 December) and (if applicable) end of each accounting period	N/A	N/A
IHT (a) Estates	(a) Earlier of delivery of account or 6 months after month of death	N/A	N/A
(b) PETs within 7 yrs of death	(b) 6 months after month of death	N/A	N/A
(c) Lifetime transfers	(c) Later of 6 months after month of transfer or 30 April in next tax year	N/A	N/A

Life expectation

Mean expectation of life, expressed in years, based on data for 1987-89

Age	Males	Females	Age	Males	Females	Age	Males	Females
0	72.47	78.06	35	39.29	44.29	70	10.79	14.00
1	72.20	77.65	36	38.34	43.32	71	10.25	13.34
2	71.25	76.70	37	37.39	42.35	72	9.73	12.68
3	70.28	75.73	38	36.44	41.39	73	9.23	12.04
4	69.31	74.75	39	35.49	40.43	74	8.75	11.41
5	68.32	73.77	40	34.54	39.47	75	8.29	10.80
6	67.34	72.78	41	33.60	38.51	76	7.85	10.21
7	66.36	71.79	42	32.66	37.56	77	7.43	9.64
8	65.37	70.80	43	31.73	36.61	78	7.03	9.08
9	64.38	69.81	44	30.80	35.67	79	6.64	8.53
10	63.40	68.82	45	29.88	34.73	80	6.28	8.01
11	62.41	67.83	46	28.97	33.80	81	5.93	7.52
12	61.42	66.84	47	28.06	32.87	82	5.61	7.05
13	60.43	65.85	48	27.17	31.95	83	5.30	6.60
14	59.45	64.86	49	26.28	31.04	84	5.01	6.17
15	58.47	63.87	50	25.40	30.12	85	4.73	5.76
16	57.49	62.89	51	24.52	29.22	86	4.49	5.38
17	56.52	61.91	52	23.66	28.32	87	4.24	5.02
18	55.57	60.92	53	22.80	27.43	88	4.01	4.68
19	54.62	59.94	54	21.97	26.55	89	3.78	4.34
20	53.67	58.96	55	21.14	25.67	90	3.59	4.05
21	52.72	57.98	56	20.33	24.81	91	3.39	3.80
22	51.76	57.00	57	19.53	23.96	92	3.19	3.55
23	50.81	56.02	58	18.75	23.11	93	2.99	3.33
24	49.85	55.04	59	17.99	22.28	94	2.78	3.15
25	48.89	54.06	60	17.24	21.46	95	2.57	3.02
26	47.93	53.07	61	16.51	20.66	96	2.43	2.86
27	46.97	52.09	62	15.81	19.87	97	2.29	2.71
28	46.01	51.11	63	15.11	19.10	98	2.15	2.55
29	45.04	50.13	64	14.44	18.33	99	2.00	2.38
30	44.08	49.15	65	13.79	17.58	100	1.87	2.21
31	43.12	48.17	66	13.16	16.85			
32	42.16	47.20	67	12.55	16.12			
33	41.20	46.23	68	11.95	15.40			
34	40.25	45.25	69	11.35	14.69			

Index

AA table (car costs) 24
Advance Corporation Tax:
   due dates................................77
   fractions 18
Average earnings index 47

Base rates (clearing banks) 75
Beneficial loans, official rates 25

Calendars, 1992, 1993 6-7
Capital allowances, table 34
Capital duty 69
Capital Gains Tax:
   gilts table 10-11
   indexation allowance 12-17
   leases (allowable expenditure) 9
   prescribed rate (overdue tax) 39
   rates 8
   reliefs and exemptions 8
   repayment supplements 39
Capital Transfer Tax 52-55
Cars:
   AA table 24
   benefit table 23
   fixed profit car scheme 22
   fuel benefit table 22
   mobile telephone benefit 23
Certificates of tax deposit rates table ..35-36
Clearing bank base rates 75
Close company abatements 18
Corporation Tax:
   due dates 77
   marginal relief 18
   prescribed rate (overdue tax) 39
   rates 18
   repayment supplements 39
   see also *Advance Corporation Tax*
Court special account interest rates 74
Covenants 25
Customs and Excise Notices and
   Leaflets 72-73

DSS leaflets 59-60
Double tax agreements 40-43
Due dates of tax 77

Earnings cap (pensions) 26
European Community, member states 71
Exchange rates 43-45
   average rates 44-45
   year end rates 43
Extra statutory concessions:
   A1 (flat rate allowances) 31-32
   A19 (remission of tax) 38

Fixed profit car scheme 22
Flat rate allowances 31-32
Foreign emoluments deduction 28
FT-SE 100 share index 49
FT 30 share index 49

Gilt-edged securities 10-11

House price index statistics 48

Income tax:
   additional rate 19
   allowances 20-21
   beneficial loans, on 25
   car benefit 23
   car fuel benefit 22
   covenants 25
   due dates 77
   flat rate allowances 31-32
   foreign emoluments, on 28
   personal pension schemes, and 26
   prescribed rate (overdue tax) 39
   rates.....................................19
   reliefs 20-21
   repayment supplements 39
   retirement annuities 26-27
   small maintenance payments 25
   Schedule D Cases IV and V 28
   Schedule E 28
   uniform allowances 33
   wife's earnings election 22
Indexation allowance 12-17
Industrial buildings allowances - see *Capital allowances*
Inheritance Tax:
   due dates 77
   prescribed rate (overdue tax) 39
   rates 50-51
   reliefs and exemptions 50
   repayment supplements 39
Inland Revenue tax guides 29-30
Interest factor tables 37-38
Interest rates:
   base rates (clearing banks) 75
   beneficial loans, official rate, on 25
   overdue tax, prescribed rate on 39
   court special account, on 74
   judgment debt, on 75
   repayment supplements 39

Judgment debt interest rates 75

Life expectation table 78

Motor vehicles - see *Cars*
Multiplier tables 76

National insurance:
   benefits, taxable and non-taxable .56, 58
   contribution rates 61-66
   DSS leaflets 59-60
   statutory sick and maternity pay 57

Partnership retirement annuities 27
Personal pension schemes 26
Plant and machinery - see *Capital allowances*

Remission of tax 38
Repayment supplements 39
Retail Prices Index 46
    See also *Indexation allowance*
Retirement:
    ages, early 26
    annuities 26-27

Small companies marginal relief 18
Small maintenance payments 25
Special damage interest table 74
Stamp duties:
    ad valorem rates 67
    capital duty 69
    exempt instruments 68-69
    fixed duties (surviving and repealed) .67
    reliefs 69
    reserve tax 69

Tax deposit certificates 35-36
Tax treaties - see *Double tax agreements*
Trusts, additional rate on 19

Uniform allowances 33

Value Added Tax:
    exempt supplies 70
    Notices and leaflets 72-73
    rates.................................70
    registration and de-registration limits 71
    reverse charge services 70
    zero-rated supplies 70

Wife's earnings election 22